The Christian School: An Introduction

Noel Weeks

The Banner of Truth Trust

THE BANNER OF TRUTH TRUST
3 Murrayfield Road, Edinburgh EH 12 6EL
PO Box 621, Carlisle, Pennsylvania 17013, USA

★

© Noel Weeks 1988
First published 1988
ISBN 0 85151 526 6
Scripture quotations are from the New
American Standard Bible, © 1960, 1962,
1963, 1968, 1971, 1972, 1973, 1975, 1977 by
The Lockman Foundation. Used by permission.

★

Typeset in 10½/12pt. Linotron Plantin at The Spartan Press Limited,
Lymington, Hants
Reproduced, printed and bound in Great Britain by
Hazell Watson & Viney Limited
Member of BPCC plc
Aylesbury, Bucks, England

CONTENTS

Acknowledgements		vii
Introduction		ix
1	Why Schooling?	1
2	Rationalism and Education	16
3	Romanticism and Education	28
4	The Social Role of the School	48
5	Teaching	61
6	Relationships within the School Community	77
7	Evangelism and the Christian School	95
8	History	106
9	Science	123
10	Language	138
11	Literature	148
12	Mathematics	161
13	Other Areas	168
14	Conclusion	175
Appendix: A Curriculum Sample		178
Index		199

ACKNOWLEDGEMENTS

This book is the product of a community: the Sutherland Shire Parent-Controlled Christian School. The thoughts are my own but they have been shaped and refined by interaction with that group of parents, teachers and pupils. They are too many to name individually, so I record here my debt to the group.

Some people outside that group made major contributions. Miss Lisa Ochocki typed the manuscript. Mr Larry Sabine read the manuscript and made comments and criticisms. Mr S. M. Houghton made many helpful suggestions. Mr David Cummings of the Christian Education Association offered much advice and encouragement. I am also grateful to John Muether, the librarian of Westminster Seminary, for producing the index.

INTRODUCTION

THE CONTEXT

This book grew out of the establishment and operation of a Parent-Controlled Christian School in the southern suburbs of Sydney, N.S.W., Australia. In many ways it will reflect that Australian context. The educational ideas and movements considered will be those which have had an impact in Australian education. They may not be as prominent or may appear under somewhat different forms and labels elsewhere in the world. Nevertheless the biblical principles developed in the discussion remain valid for other situations.

THE READERSHIP

The circle of people concerned with education is very wide. Parents obviously have one concern and teachers a related but slightly different interest. Teachers may also be parents.

People vary in their exposure to the Christian school movement. Some may have merely heard of it and be concerned largely for what it means for the Christian presence in the state school. Others may desire such a school but be uncertain as to the form it should take. Others again may be actively involved but have questions on matters of organization or curriculum.

It is very hard to answer the questions and meet the concerns of as diverse an audience as this. We beg the reader's consideration if there is not more treatment of the particular questions of most concern to him or her.

EMPHASES AND OMISSIONS

Initially this book was conceived as an outline of Christian school curriculum. That was because the need we perceived was in this area. As the book developed and we consulted with others the scope grew wider. It became clear that curriculum could not be developed or explained without first explaining the difference between a biblical position and the philosophical movements that influence modern education.

There has been no conscious attempt to deal with the role of the Christian teaching in a state school. The omission should not be read as disapproval. We thoroughly support a strong and distinctive witness by Christian teachers in state schools. The omission is because the whole book is written from the perspective of parents. We are concerned to assist parents in their God-given task of raising their children in the fear and nurture of the Lord.

CURRICULUM

Our school does not publish educational materials. We have done some work in developing curriculum. We would stress that this material is not of the level of a commercial production and has many gaps. Nevertheless if it would be of use to any others who are struggling with the problems of curriculum development, we shall be glad to make it available for the cost of production and postage.

Similarly we are concerned to learn also from others and would welcome insights on Christian school organization and curriculum.

Please write to: Sutherland Shire Christian School,
P.O. Box 390,
Sutherland,
N.S.W.,
Australia, 2232.

৩৩ I ৩৩

Why Schooling?

Schooling of some sort is an accepted part of our societies. There are critics who question the institution, but on the whole schools tend to be accepted as a necessary part of life. Yet the fact that they are accepted does not mean that there is universal agreement about their purpose. If a poll were taken a majority of the populace would probably describe their purpose as preparation for later gainful employment. A significant group of educators might be more likely to talk in terms of their role in equipping the child to function in society. An economist might be more concerned with their function in keeping youth out of the work force and allowing mothers to join the work force.

Different ideas of the purpose of a school will lead to different approaches to education. We see in most schools a compromise between various approaches. Hence the differences may not be obvious. Yet they exist.

What of the Christian? Does he have a particular understanding of schooling? It has to be confessed that he generally does not. He accepts the vague ideas and unformulated thoughts of society at large. Even when Christian schools have been founded, their purpose is not always seen in a particularly clear way.

THE BIBLE AND CHILDREN

Part of the problem is that the Bible does not mention schools. Hence Christians have a tendency to accept what is believed and practised in the society around them. Many of them are quite at a loss to bring biblical ideas to bear on the whole question of education.

[1]

Yet the Bible does say some things about the raising of children. Let us work out the implications of its teachings.

In both the Old Testament and the New Testament the responsibility for the training of children is placed upon the parents. We can cite as typical passages from each Testament Deuteronomy 6:4–7 and Ephesians 6:4. There are a number of major concerns in such passages.

1. The goal of training is godliness. This comes through also as a major theme in the Book of Proverbs. Proverbs is in the form of instruction from the parents to the child. That instruction seeks to preserve the child from the common sins of the world.

2. The training is comprehensive in its scope. That idea is conveyed most effectively by Deuteronomy 6:4–7. The parent is to talk about the law of God, 'when you sit in your house and when you walk by the way and when you lie down and when you rise up.' That is, all the time. There is no part of the day's activities upon which the truth of God does not impinge.

This may come as an unusual thought to those used to the compartmentalization of 'religion' in modern society. The Old Testament law knew no such compartmentalization. It touched on all the aspects of Israelite life: social relationships, agriculture, commerce, building, sanitation, and many more. Hence the training of the child must be comprehensive.

3. It combines discipline and love. While the Bible warns against arbitrary harshness (e.g. Eph. 6:4) it also encourages discipline (Prov. 13:24; 22:15; 23: 13, 14).

4. Teaching is to be done by one who has absorbed the truth of God. The law is first to be in the heart of the parent (Deut. 6:6, 7). Formal times of instruction may be observed by somebody who does not have God's law in his heart. Only the person who has absorbed it will speak of it naturally in all the varying situations of life.

Note that the Bible does not have some of the dichotomies that characterize contemporary approaches to education. It is a training in godliness and yet that training touches every aspect of life. It does not set discipline against love. The revealed law of God gives education content but the existence of a block of authoritative material does not make instruction purely formal. Rather it stimulates informal education.

Many contemporary educators would turn these things into

dilemmas or contradictions. A Christian education is for them synonymous with a narrow education. Love and discipline are held to be mutually exclusive. It is argued that only if we abandon all notion of an authoritative basis for education can we have instruction that goes beyond the stilted and the formal. Discussion and dialogue can occur only if there is no certain truth.

CHILDREN AND THE CHURCH

Whenever Scripture singles out people as responsible for the training of children it places that responsibility upon parents. That does not mean that the church has no responsibility to teach children. The church has a responsibility to teach persons of all ages, including children. The New Testament letters, written to be read in the congregation, contain sections addressed to children. That presupposes that children would be present in the meetings of the congregation.

However, when both Testaments deal specifically with the training of children, then they give the parents that task. Hence in thinking through the training and schooling of children we have to start with the role of parents.

THE BIBLE AND SCHOOLS

The Bible does not mention the training of children through schools. That has led to various Christian assessments of the whole institution of schooling. Some argue that we should not send children to school but rather teach them at home. Others argue that the Bible does not mention schools because there were no schools in biblical times. We now have schools because the great increase in knowledge since biblical times makes parental education impracticable. Hence the biblical material on the raising of children is fundamentally irrelevant to our advanced times. The very reverse of this second argument has also been presented. It is that there were schools in biblical times: village schools, synagogue schools, or schools in the pagan societies of New Testament times. Since there are no commands for believers to withdraw their children from such schools, we presume they continued to attend schools which were not specifically Christian. They may have been Jewish schools or the pagan schools that the children of Gentiles attended. The implication is that if New Testament believers were not concerned about their children receiving an education hostile to their faith, then neither should Christian parents of the present be concerned.

We thus have three arguments with very different conclusions. While the second and third arguments differ on the historical question of whether there were schools for children in biblical times, they come to very similar conclusions, namely, that Christians should accept uncritically the existing institutions of schooling. In effect they blunt the force of the biblical admonitions to parents. Whereas the concern of Deuteronomy 6 was that the whole life of the child be surrounded with the truth that springs from God's revelation, these arguments urge us to accept the existing educational institutions, whether Christian or not.

Can we use the existence of something the Bible does not even mention, to put aside what the Bible sets before us? The whole argument from the lack of mention of schools in the Bible has all the problems of arguments from silence. There are many gaps in our historical knowledge about schools. We have very little evidence on schools in Palestine in Old Testament times. That does not mean that they did not exist. Schools existed to train scribes in other countries of the time. But these countries had much more difficult scripts and it is doubtful if we can argue from them to the situation in Israel. Our knowledge of early synagogues is minimal. We may make mistakes reasoning from the situation in the synagogue long after New Testament times. We are on somewhat firmer ground with schools in pagan societies in New Testament times. Yet what we do not know is the extent of Christian involvement in those schools. We can even assume for the sake of the argument that Gentiles when converted left their children in pagan schools, for people, when they become Christians, are not instantly transported into an ideal world. There is a process, sometimes a long process, of readjustment, transformation and change. In towns in which the church has only just been formed, and in which people have only just begun to make the changes that follow confession of Jesus as Lord, can we realistically expect a Christian school to begin overnight? Where would the teachers be found?

If we had a specific biblical command either for parents to withdraw their children from pagan schools, or for them not to withdraw them, then we would have something concrete. We have neither. Hence we have to try to work out the implications of what we actually find in Scripture. Our conclusions may differ from those of the church in the first couple of centuries after New Testament times. If they do, then education will not be the only matter on which we disagree with the ancient church.

HOME SCHOOLING AND THE INCOMPETENCE OF PARENTS

The arguments over the relevance of Scripture to education span the range between those who want a return to the education of children by parents and those who argue for the incompetence of parents in matters of education. Obviously those who argue that parents should educate their own children are trying to take seriously the biblical teaching. Those who argue for the incompetence of parents claim that the advances of knowledge, in practice, rule out the possibility of home education. Of the parents who possess the relevant knowledge, very few have the requisite ability, or the necessary time, to act as teachers.

The argument for home schooling can be variously presented. One could argue for taking the whole education of children back into the home. Or one can argue that the attempt should be made to arrange at least for younger children to receive education at home. It is often conceded that it is hard, in practice, to conduct high school education at home.

How do we decide this debate? However we decide it, there are several things we must not do. We must not use our supposed incompetence or lack of time as an excuse for disobedience to a biblical command. If we have problems and difficulties in obeying the commandment, then we should seek ways to overcome them. Our responsibilities as parents cannot be simply brushed aside.

Is it true that parents are incompetent to educate their children? We can always think of cases in which that may be true, but is it universally true? A moment's reflection will indicate that it is not so. If we confine ourselves to the very early years of schooling, then it would be quite within the ability of most parents. Some educators have built a mystique around education to justify their own employment to train teachers. This will be considered later. However if we do not accept that education is some deep secret that people can only acquire via a special course labelled 'education', then we would say that most parents could teach their children. They may have to do a little study themselves but they could do it.

The greater problem is time. This problem particularly concerns fathers. For while Scripture does refer to the role of both parents in training the child (Prov. 1:8) there is a definite tendency to place particular responsibility on the father (e.g. Eph. 6:4). We might wish for a return to a situation in which small farming or cottage industry gave men time to be with their families while working and considerable flexibility in their hours of work. Though it may seem like an impossible dream, we as Christians need to think and work towards a work style that is more conducive to family life.

However, in the interim, we must find a way of reconciling our need to work to support our families and our need to train our children comprehensively in the ways of the Lord. Mothers can fill some of that gap but they will not fill all of it.

When we as Christians have difficulty in meeting our responsibilities we naturally turn to our fellow believers for help. It is part of our sharing of one another's burdens. Suppose two Christian mothers were both teaching their children at home. One met with difficulty in teaching mathematics but possessed musical abilities. The other had the reverse problem. Would it not be the natural thing for them to arrange the teaching so that their strong points could be shared?

A Christian school is based on this process of sharing carried out on a much larger scale. It has to be admitted that most Christian schools do not reach this ideal. There is a strong tendency for them to ape the state schools in which the parents effectively hand over the children to the 'expert' teacher and have no say or role in education. Most Christian schools need far greater parental involvement.

However, that does not affect the real justification for such schools. The plain fact is that they provide a co-operative way in which parents acting together can achieve what they could not achieve alone. While the basic idea is one of a co-operative of parents, there is no reason why the parent should not enlist the aid of an unmarried member of the Christian community. Of course, once you start asking fellow Christians to engage in services to help you, you place yourself under responsibility to remunerate them. The labourer is worthy of his hire.

[6]

THE NATURE OF A CHRISTIAN SCHOOL

A school which develops to meet the needs and responsibilities outlined above will have certain characteristics. Fundamentally it exists to aid parents in their task of raising children in the fear of the Lord. That focuses the education into certain channels.

1. It is supplementary. The school does not monopolize the child's whole education for it exists to be a help and adjunct to what the family itself is doing in the education of its children. A school which tries to assume full responsibility for the training of children will compete with the family. The most obvious way in which it will compete will be in regard to 'time'. One needs to ask whether a school which sticks to its proper task would need to impose excessive homework on pupils which can cut into their time with the family.

2. It will supplement what the parents are required to do. That is, it will apply the truth of God to every circumstance of the child's life. It will not engage in a purely formal set of religious exercises or lessons divorced from the rest of the curriculum.

3. Parents are to train their children. Training implies a goal. That is, there is an objective towards which they are moving, one of Christian maturity. Christian maturity has many aspects and phases. Some of these are mentioned in Ephesians 4:14, 15. Paul mentions that children are easily deceived and swayed. Maturity involves a knowledge of the truth and the ability to communicate it in love. Obviously much of the teaching of love and truth has to be done in the home. The school can supplement but it cannot replace the home.

4. Various skills, for example, reading, writing, and speaking, are necessary if we are to know and communicate the truth. A school can play a role in extending the home instruction of such skills. However, it must never be for the sake of the skills themselves. It must always be with a view to a contribution to that ultimate goal: the building up of the body of Christ.

5. Some of the skills which contribute to this growth are also useful in the earning of an income. Generally speaking, the ability to earn an income is a goal for which parents train children. It is a Christian goal, for the Christian is to strive to provide for his family and to give to those in need. In some recent educational debate, training for remunerative work has been a contentious issue.

[7]

There are those who think the school should develop the personality of the child, not simply prepare him to be another number in the work force statistics. Aspects of this debate will be considered later. For the moment it can be said that from the Christian perspective the terms of the debate are wrong. We must not encourage the idea that the full flowering of human personality and potential, and the needs of work and employment are contraries. Man's real fulfilment lies in service that contributes to the growth of others. To do this he needs certain skills, for instance, the ability to speak the truth in love. That skill will also assist him in earning a living. Moreover if he approaches his work and his earnings correctly, then in that work and from that work he will further contribute to the advancement of the kingdom of God.

6. In the nature of the case the home may be better fitted to train a child in one aspect of his development and the school in another. A parent who is with the child constantly in the informal situations of the home may be far better placed to teach a child patience and self-control than a school teacher. But obviously a school with the requisite equipment may be more efficient in applying that patience to the acquiring of skills in carpentry or science.

7. While the school may contribute to the development of a child's personality or help in the management of personal relationships, it is quite unable to replace the parent in this training. It is better for both parents and school that the school spends its time doing what it can do well and allows parent and child more time together to achieve what comes best out of that relationship. Hence there is a very important point to be grasped. A school has to allocate time to the things it can do. Some more important things may be passed over because in those matters a school is not effective. A school system which refuses to recognize those limitations is a danger to the family, not a help to it.

THE STRENGTHS AND WEAKNESSES OF A SCHOOL

A school is not well equipped to deal with personal problems and problems of behaviour which require a long term relationship between a mature Christian adult and a child. That is solely because the teacher seldom has time to develop such relationships. Many teachers do contribute by being willing to give that extra time. Often they give of themselves sacrificially to make up for what a parent could have done but has not done. Nevertheless the parent is better placed for this task.

The school functions most efficiently when it imparts skills or knowledge which can be taught in a group situation. Now much of contemporary educational thought is opposed to teaching classes as a whole. The reasons for this will be discussed more extensively later. Nevertheless it remains true that what the school does best is to take the knowledge and ability resident in one adult and to transmit that to a number of children. It is more efficient in the sense that a special expertise, which maybe not one of the thirty or so fathers represented in the class could have taught his child, has now been acquired by those children. It is more efficient in that employing one person to impart that ability is cheaper than employing one for each child. Finally, if the teacher is a good teacher, there will be an economy of time. A teacher who can train children quickly leaves time for the child to learn more and mature more.

Knowing this we will shape our curriculum to do what a school does best. We must not waste the child's and thus the family's time in doing what a school does least effectively.

AN EXAMPLE

It is obvious to most people that a child's difficulty in learning is often attitudinal and behavioural. It is also obvious that the difficulty some people have in obtaining and holding adequate employment is closely related to these educational problems.

There seems an obvious answer. The school should devote itself to teaching behaviour and attitudes, even if this means ignoring its other academic functions.

How can a school accomplish this? The best way would be the way parents accomplish it. It would be to work with each child in individual discussion and counselling, but with an adult setting an example of a positive attitude to study and work. Could any school system afford to assign a counsellor to each child? An additional problem would be the fact that what the school attempted to do might well be undone once the child went home and was exposed to contrasting approaches. The basic problem is that the child rarely forms a bond with a teacher strong enough to compensate, for good or ill, with the bond between child and parent.

[9]

THE CHRISTIAN SCHOOL: AN INTRODUCTION

There have been schools which have attempted to shift the main thrust of their activities into these areas of attitudes and behaviour. As will be discussed later some of the recent shifts in educational thinking are influenced by this concern. Nevertheless they wrestle with a fundamental problem. Attitudes are very much shaped by the home. How can the school replace the home?

A popular way of doing this is by trying to make the child an autonomous, reasoning, decision-making individual. The theory is that if the the child is taught that he has to make his own decisions and that nobody can make them for him, he will become a mature, responsible, reasoning adult. The theory rarely works and for an obvious reason. The idea of an autonomous person sabotages the relation the child has with his parents. That relationship is not just a relationship of reason. It is an emotional relationship in which the parent provides a model to be emulated. The child without that emotional relationship is in difficulty. If the school destroys that relationship it really has nothing to put in its place. The teacher who is teaching his pupils to take the detached attitude of critical reason is not simultaneously going to be exercising loving and protective leadership. He will not set an example to be followed of warm personal relationships. His very theory militates against him seeing himself as a parent figure to the child.

This is not to argue that a school should not teach a pupil to think and reason. Indeed it should do so. It is simply saying that there is more to being a responsible adult than critical reason. There are all the other attributes of full human personality. A school that accepts those other attributes which are most naturally learned by imitation of parents, and supports them, will do more to foster adult maturity than one which undermines the parental model.

The problems thrown up by this discussion remind us that, basically, the school is not a home. When it tries completely to replace the home, knowingly or unknowingly, it undermines the home. A good example of this is the teaching that a child should be autonomous, accepting no outside authority because there are no real and certain values. Obviously this challenges the parents' right to say to that child, 'You must do this or that because it is right'.

On the other hand the school can act as a complement to the home. Then it does what it does best and allows the home to fulfil its proper function without interference.

THE SCHOOL AND THE BAD HOME

Many educators, particularly secular ones, will object to this argument. They will object that it presupposes good homes. Many pupils do not come from good homes. In that situation the school has no choice but to attempt to replace the home. 'Surely', they would argue, 'it is better to teach the child to reason for himself, than to leave him blindly following a bad home example.'

A further question must be answered. What constitutes a bad home and what are the values which should be substituted for those of the parents? In an age of relativism this is a difficult question to answer. As already outlined above, the common answer is that the child must autonomously work out his values for himself. This then attacks the authority of all the homes that are not bad. In seeking to correct the bad homes the school weakens the better ones.

Actually the secular educator is being quite illogical. If there are not absolutes, how can a home or a child's attitudes and behaviour be labelled as 'bad'? It does not help to say it is not 'bad', just 'inappropriate' or 'anti-social'. You need to have some standard or else you would decide that inappropriate or anti-social behaviour is quite acceptable. However, to acknowledge a standard of judgment would undermine the secular educator's claim to be religiously neutral. So in hypocrisy he devises relativistic curricula to deal with homes which, in his moral judgment, he claims to be bad. Of course, for a true relativist, a home which teaches the absolutes of God's Word may be a very bad home.

Yet the fact remains that somebody not dedicated to relativism will raise the reality of poor homes. Is the school to ignore this problem?

The real question is, How can the school best contribute to alleviating the damage caused by a bad home? It will not necessarily be by removing the child totally from connection with that home. The debate still rages amongst social workers as to whether it is best to remove a child from a very bad home environment. Obviously sometimes it has to be done for the physical safety of the child. Nevertheless the record of children removed from bad home situations to alternatives is not good. There is a simple reason. The family is a divine institution. The child needs parents to whom he can relate. Removal to an alternative situation can be very confusing to the child. To whom does he relate? This is not to deny that foster parents are sometimes most successful. It is simply to say that it is difficult for child and foster parent alike.

Actually, what we would all like to see is the bad home made good. We would like to see the child's influence acting as a positive force for good in his home. A child is responsible before God to honour his parents. If they are bad parents the task may be made harder but the responsibility is not removed. For many children growing up in bad homes, the trial of having to honour parents is a crucial test to be passed on the road to genuine maturity.

Naturally one may ask why such a child would want to honour his parents. He will do so if he is convinced that God commands it. That fact brings us back to the question of the role of the school. As an extension of the family the Christian school reflects some of the structures and dynamics of a family. There is love on the part of teachers and respect on the part of pupils. If the child does not experience such a relationship in his own home, then experiencing it at school gives him some taste of proper relationships. Certainly the attitudes taught in the home will compete with those taught in school. Nevertheless the Christian school does possess one advantage denied to the secular school. It is able to say that what it sets forth as proper relationships is what God requires. Not all pupils will understand this. However, under the influence of the Spirit of God a child may accept it. He then becomes a positive influence for good in the home.

The secular school, in setting out to replace the home, must fail in its positive goal of helping bad homes. The Christian school in reflecting the dynamics of a good home and supplementing the home has a greater hope for success.

Let us return to the point raised much earlier about attitudes to work. Ideally the parents are the models for such attitudes. But suppose that they are bad examples. Let us further take two contrasting ways in which a teacher might deal with this problem. One teacher recognizes the problem. He seeks to meet it by discussing the question of work attitudes in class. He is careful not to impose his views on the class but tries to stimulate the pupils to think through and develop their own philosophy of work. Another teacher also recognizes the problem. He seeks to meet it by taking a positive attitude to his own work and by making the pupils work hard so that they can experience the satisfaction of accomplishment. He encounters resistance from pupils who have not been encouraged to work at home. He seeks to meet this by encouraging his pupils to persevere and by pointing out that what he requires is not more than what God requires.

Anybody who rejects the Word of God might favour the first approach. There are few other reasons for favouring it. The pupils are left without direction or reasons for change in their behaviour. The approach is quite theoretical. The pupils are not exposed to work or the satisfaction of work well done. They do not see a model who works and enjoys it.

Perhaps we could suggest taking one good point out of each approach. The school might see its main task as training children in right attitudes to work and in correct behaviour. If the children have the right attitude, then the learning of actual skills will be very easy and need not occupy the school's time. The difference from the example considered earlier is that this teaching on attitudes would be directive and done from a Christian point of view.

The question raised by this example is whether a Christian school should see itself as essentially training in attitudes, with the premise that once the attitudes are well established other things follow naturally. There is an element of truth in this premise. Often, attitudes are the most difficult things to teach. However, more than just attitudes must be taught. Scripture does stress attitudes. It also stresses that those attitudes must be shown and tested in deeds. It is one thing to say that our pupils now have the right attitudes; it is another thing for them to prove it in the work they do. Often the person who thinks his attitude is right finds it is not so when he has to work in situations which are discouraging. On a level appropriate to the child's age and maturity, the child has to learn to put attitudes into practice.

A teacher may find that he cannot settle down to work with the children until he has dealt with their bad attitudes. He may be able to set them to work but soon discovers that the discipline of work reveals problems in their approach to it. The attitude to work and the work itself must both be set before the pupil.

The approach which sees the mental attitude as the only thing to be taught will come up again when we discuss rationalism. For the moment it suffices to say that it sees the problem as purely mental and theoretical. It ignores the difficulties of self-discipline and self-control for children. We all can be mentally convinced we should do this or that and yet not do it when it proves difficult.

Some readers may be wondering why we introduce the discussion of bad homes in connection with a Christian school. For they assume that only strong Christian homes would send their children to a Christian school. Some schools have adopted enrolment policies which attempt to ensure this to be the case. Enrolment policy is not the issue for the moment here. However, even granting such an enrolment policy, it rarely prevents the school from having to confront such problems. Regrettably, Christian homes are not always good homes. The family may be newly converted and have a legacy of years of problems. One parent may be an unbeliever. In the world as we find it, the school which is not equipped to cope with students with poor home backgrounds will have problems.

There is another reason why Christian schools must face this issue. Educational theory and practice today is not being developed with Christian homes in mind. It often assumes the failure of the home. Christian educators tend to be influenced by what is dominant in the educational world in general. Unless we develop our own approach to the problem of poor homes, we shall ourselves assume the validity of the approach developed by secular educators.

RESUMÉ

Why do we have schools? We have them not because we assume the home is incompetent. We have them to assist and extend the ministry of parents. Their goal and curriculum are alike determined by what is needed to supplement the parents' teaching; not by any abstract theory or principle which approaches education as though the parents could be ignored.

Yet even when the home from which the child comes is far from strong, the approach devised to supplement the strong home is applicable, the reason being that it extends and mirrors what is done in the Christian home. The model that is then set before the

Why Schooling?

child is the model he has been denied at home. There is a relationship of loving authority. God's Word is used to illuminate and direct all that is done. The child is required to work according to the way the Bible teaches. And this is all supported by the belief that it is the will of God as revealed in his Word.

∾ 2 ∾

Rationalism and Education

TWO IMPORTANT INFLUENCES

It is hard to break loose completely from our culture and background. Even when we are proclaiming that we have a radically Christian form of education we may carry much of the baggage of secular education into our schools. Hence it is important to identify major non-Christian approaches to education. We need to supply a Christian critique of these approaches.

There are certain dangers in this approach. There is the danger that we shall assume that whatever is contrary to a particular non-Christian approach is necessarily Christian. Quite often non-Christian schools of thought are sharply opposed to one another. Merely to take a different position from a particular school will not necessarily put us in a Christian position. It may put us in another secular one.

Hence it is important to realize that there is more than one form of non-Christian educational theory. In fact there are several. This chapter and the next will deal with two major influences on education which are opposed to each other on many points. It is an opposition which generates much of the so-called 'debate' in education. In their opposition to a Christian position, however, they show a large measure of agreement. Hence, as already mentioned, we cannot simply think that what is opposed to one variety of non-Christian thought is necessarily Christian. Nor can we fall back on the idea that truth resides at the point where all major educationalists agree. That may simply be the consensus of non-Christian thought.

The two major influences to be considered are rationalism and romanticism. The history of their influence and their interaction is

[16]

complex and our treatment of them will involve a certain amount of simplification. Put simply, rationalism is likely to have been a major influence in the education of the older generation. Quite often, calls for a return to the old ways in education are virtually calls for a resurgence of rationalism. In more recent times rationalism has been strongly challenged by romanticism. What are called new educational 'insights' are likely to be undiluted romanticism.

Within the contemporary domain of education, rationalism and romanticism compete in other ways. There is a tendency for rationalism to be more dominant in high school education while romanticism has a stronger hold over infant education. The sciences lean more to rationalism while the humanities, and especially the fine arts, reflect more romanticism.

All these are generalizations and have the problems of generalizations. Nevertheless they may help the reader to identify these influences as he has encountered them, for one of the problems is that proponents of such trends are reluctant to identify their allegiance. They do not proclaim that they see the world in terms of a certain philosophy and want to impose that philosophy on education. They use all sorts of secondary arguments to promote their educational theories.

THE RATIONALIST TEMPER

As it influences education, rationalism may be a tendency and a temper as much as it is a rigorous philosophical position. It is a way of understanding the relationship of man's mind to the world around. The person with such a viewpoint may be unaware of his philosophical allegiance. To him it is a self-evident position. In reality it has become part of his religious vision and hope. Yet he seldom realizes why he holds that vision.

Hence the definition of rationalism in education may be somewhat different from a definition of pure philosophical rationalism. The crucial belief is that the mind of man is capable of exhaustive knowledge of the whole of reality.

To those used to philosophical exactitude this definition will be too vague. For example, it could be made to cover rationalists in the more traditional philosophical sense and also empiricists. Traditionally the distinction between these two positions is that rationalists put emphasis upon the reasoning and deductions of the human mind as the way to the truth. The empiricists tend to stress more what man's senses tell him about things around him.

Yet what penetrates into education and comes to expression in a textbook or an educational approach, generally does not draw such distinctions. It is likely to stress both reasoning and observation. What makes it rationalist is the conviction that the world can all be exhaustively known and understood by man.

THE FACTS

A consequence of this belief is the conviction that knowledge consists of a set of facts. Education is the impartation of those facts. When man has learned all these facts he will have perfect knowledge. The facts are believed to exist in a relationship which is understandable to man.

This belief shapes what is considered to be knowledge. What cannot be easily packaged as factual and placed in relationship is not considered. A few simple examples may make this approach easier to visualize. In these examples other factors may have shaped the approach but they still illustrate a rationalist temper. Why has history been taught in terms of the names of rulers and the dates of battles and other events? These are concrete facts. History can then be organized in terms of the structure given by a sense of dates. The rulers and the battles are the important 'facts'. Thus the approach determines what constitutes the important material to be learned. Another example would be the teaching of geography in terms of the names of countries, cities, rivers, etc. These are concrete and factual. Knowledge of them gives structure to geography.

The empiricist may place the emphasis more upon how man discovers these facts. The traditional rationalist will be more concerned with finding the order which exists amongst these facts. Nevertheless there is a similar basic conviction. The facts are as the mind of secular man discovers them. There is nothing uncertain or requiring qualification in man's knowledge of these facts.

When pressed, the rationalist will qualify his bold claims. He will say that there is much that yet remains for man to discover. He will admit that later discoveries will cause a modification of what is claimed as fact today. Nevertheless he is confident that he has the correct method and approach to discover and arrange these additional facts.

Remaining uncertainties, however, do not influence rationalist approaches to education. The facts are presented to the children as absolutely certain and unquestioned. And it is not only the case that the rationalist version of the facts is presented so dogmatically. The whole framework of rationalist thought is presented as unquestionably true. It is assumed that sinful man, with his unaided reason, is fully capable of comprehending the facts and placing them in the correct relationship to one another. Often it is the method for discovery of the facts that is presented with this dogmatic certainty, whether by the method of empirical scientific investigation or the method of critical reflection on what has been discovered about the world around us.

PRELIMINARY CRITIQUE

Many will ask what is wrong with the rationalist approach to knowledge and hence to education, and will do so partly because this approach to facts is very commonly accepted in our culture. They will also put forward their query because the scientific approach seems to have produced so many discoveries.

This apparent success of non-Christian science creates a general question for Christians. How can a method and approach which ignores God as Creator of the world be so successful in investigating the world and utilizing the knowledge thus acquired?

First we should remember that we are probably not the first to face such questions. It is striking that the biblical record of man's earliest history attributes many major discoveries to the line that came from Cain (Genesis 4). In Cain, the first of the line, and in Lamech, the last recorded, we have rebellion against God, pride and cruelty. The history of this line is in contrast to the line of Seth in which men call upon the name of the Lord (4:26), walk with God (5:22–24) and find favour in God's eyes (6:8).

Yet the line of Cain produced innovators with respect to cities, nomadic herding, musical instruments, and working in metal. It is part of the plan of Genesis to record first the history of the rejected line before it gives the history of the chosen line that leads to the promised seed. Commonly the rejected line seems to have blessings denied to the elect. Thus Ishmael had many sons

(Genesis 25:12–16). Esau's descendants were settled in their land long before Israel (Gen. 36:31). It seems as though the blessings promised to the children of the promise are given, instead, to the other line.

So also with the line of Cain. Accomplishment and success seemed to mark that line. How was that success possible? The text tells us. God restrains the punishment which they deserve. Cain deserved to die and yet his life was preserved. When Cain feared that other brothers of Abel might avenge Abel's blood, God even marked him out for special protection. Here we see God's mercy and gifts bestowed on men who do nothing to deserve it. However, the pride and violence typified by Lamech (4:23, 24) grew until it filled the earth (6:11) and the time for the long-delayed judgment came (6:5–7).

So also today we find men living in a world God has made, utilizing his gifts and enjoying his forbearance. Much of what they discover may be used by the people of God, just as the Old Testament saw nothing necessarily wrong with cities, musical instruments, nomadic herding, and metal work. However, the discoveries are in our day once again the occasions of pride and violence. And once again God's judgment must surely come.

However, we do not have to accept the attitude and interpretation of those who make these innovations any more than we have to accept the views of a Cain or a Lamech. The Scripture is quite emphatic about the state of those who refuse to acknowledge the true God. Rather than interpret the evidence aright they have missed the basic fact. God is Creator (Rom. 1:18–23). The rationalist often believes that there is something superior about man's intellect. But Romans 1 tells us that men have refused to use their minds. They have blotted out from them the knowledge of the truth. The real unwillingness to use the mind is not what the rationalist imagines. It is not a failure to think in a secular, rationalistic way. It is a wilful rejection of what is obvious from the world around us.

Man is then forced, by his unbelief of clear evidence, to propose foolish alternatives to the true God. In choosing these he loses all basis for proper rational thinking. He becomes foolish. So the mind of man is in darkness (Romans 1:21; Ephesians 2:3). From this darkness springs further corruption (Romans 1:24–32).

The outcome is that we cannot trust the products of the mind of man. Certainly man lives in and works with a world God has created. To the extent he confines himself to describing that world, he seems theoretically able to reach the truth. However, always, to a greater or lesser degree, there is the bias produced by unbelief. He must distort the truth lest that truth lead him to the true God.

THE RATIONALIST HOPE

Before continuing the critique, the world-view, or perhaps one could better say the religious hope, of rationalism must be examined in more detail. The hope is a general one which has specific application to education.

a) *General*

If man's mind is potentially capable of understanding everything in the universe, then man is potentially capable of controlling everything. Man would then have the power of God.

This approach often manifests itself in forms of reductionism. A typical approach would see man's religious and moral problems as symptoms of a lack of psychological adjustment. Man's psychological problems can, in turn, be understood through viewing man as an animal. Supposedly, we can understand man if we have comprehensive knowledge of animal behaviour and its chemical basis. Man's behaviour can then be changed by changing the chemical behaviour in his brain. To be able to understand and to control the chemistry of man's body gives promise of ability to correct all man's health and psychological problems. Chemistry can further be seen as understandable in terms of the basic laws of physics.

To turn the process around we could argue that an understanding of the fundamental processes of physics could be turned into an understanding of chemical processes in the body. With that knowledge we could correct man's physical and mental problems. Thus all human problems are solvable by more scientific knowledge.

Reductionism of one form or another is generally involved in rationalism. In order to reach the goal of understanding all, that 'all' must be reduced to something simple or very basic. Hence rationalisms typically try to find some basic entity or system to which everything else can be reduced.

b) *In Education*

The general rationalist hope is that man can come to understand the root of all his problems. With that knowledge he can correct those problems. Thus man becomes, through knowledge, his own saviour. Since the school is the place where knowledge is conveyed, it has tremendous significance for the rationalist. It is his church.

There is a more specific influence upon the form of education itself. We have seen that the rationalist believes that all the facts may be brought into a system comprehensible to man. This system is a reduction. It is simpler than the complexity and confusion we first encounter.

It seems logical that if we could discover this simple system in which all things are in their natural relationships, then that system would be easy to learn. Since each part of the system would be logically related to every other part, there would be no need for the drudgery of memorization of unrelated material. All would be easy and simple.

This hope and belief has a powerful influence upon the rationalist and his approaches to education. It follows logically from his belief that an educational system which still invokes work and memorization cannot be the right one. Hence the search for an education where the 'right' system will make learning something which happens without effort.

While this belief in the final rational system still exerts considerable influence, there has been something of a shift in approach. There is a tendency to accentuate the search for this system and to push into the background the system itself. Partly this shift is an acknowledgment of the difficulty of producing such a system. Partly it is a product of influences to be considered later.

The fundamental confidence in the unaided power of human reason has not changed. There is still confidence in man's ability to discover all the secrets of the universe.

Another thing that has remained constant is the confidence that education, given the right system, must be easy. Hence it is claimed that if only education were turned into a search for the truth, then pupils would love school. This hope lies behind much of the propaganda that surrounds the so-called 'discovery' methods of education. The utilization of such methods will also be considered later. For the moment we simply want to draw attention to the source of the extreme faith placed in discovery learning.

a) *Order and System*

There is order in the creation. Rationalism derives its apparent plausibility from that fact. There continues to be order in creation because God in his faithfulness maintains that order. Scripture ascribes that maintenance to God's upholding of his covenant with creation (Jeremiah 33:19–22).

A covenant involves a lord who gives commands and a servant who obeys. Just so, the creation obeys the command of its Lord. If God does not change his commands, then there will not be a change in the order of creation.

It is important, however, to remember that it is God who gives the commands. There will come a time when God will give different commands to his creatures. Then the sun will be darkened instead of shining day by day (Joel 2:31; Revelation 6:12–17). When God judges, then the good gifts that his providence has provided for man are taken away.

Rationalism makes the mistake of thinking that this order and regularity resides in the creation itself. Rationalists see it as an unchangeable part of the very structure of the world. Thus God does not receive his due recognition.

One sometimes encounters versions of rationalism tinged with a superficial Christianity. It may be said that God has created this rational order, or that God has implanted unchanging laws in creation and what the scientist discovers are these laws. The problem of this approach is that God is needed for nothing more than creation. Indeed his continuing existence after the creation is a major problem. For if he stops the sun shining or in any other way changes the order that now exists, he is seen as violating the law which he himself has planted in creation. It will be asked: How can God break his own law?

Thus the rationalist wants to exploit the order and regularity which God's patience maintains in the creation. He would like to turn the very patience and regularity into an argument that a day of judgment can never come. However, Scripture tells us that we are not to misinterpret the longsuffering of God. We are to ignore the arguments of those who say that the regularity of the present order tells against any real, active divine power (2 Peter 3:1–13).

b) *The Knowledge of a Creature*

The rationalist hopes that knowledge will lead to power. If he can understand the world around him, then he can control it. In many ways this hope seems to be increasingly fulfilled. Man, with his science and technology, does just that.

For the rationalist's hope to be realized, he has to go far beyond this present stage. His desire is comprehensive knowledge and total control. In short man aspires to what God alone possesses. In the Book of Job, God ridicules such hopes. In questioning God's providential rule, Job was seeking to take on the role that is God's alone, the role of governor of the universe. Hence God asked whether it was Job who was the lord of creation. Was he the one giving commands (Job 38–41, especially 38:12, 18, 33, 34, 35)? As the rationalist correctly realizes, there is a connection between knowledge and power. If one knew and understood the ordinances of heaven one could fix their rule over all the earth or command the clouds to pour out rain. However, man's interpretation of the regularity that results from God's covenant with creation is not the same as the commands God actually utters. We may perceive some of that order and the interconnections between parts of the universe. That is not the same as speaking to creation and having it obey you.

In other words, we could say quite simply that man is not God. Man can use and depend upon order in creation. He cannot make it or change it. The way God's command preserves such order is a mystery to man.

c) *Sin and Knowledge*

The previous section concerned the knowledge man has as a creature. Man is also a sinner and sin has an effect on the mind. The rationalist correctly realizes that any marring of the human mind will destroy his whole system. Hence much of the rationalist attack on Christianity is devoted to this very point. The achievements of science are produced as evidence of the greatness of the human mind. Such achievements may be remarkable but are they intrinsically different from the achievements of the line of Cain? Man may use his abilities as a creature, and the regularities of the creation, to accomplish much. Yet as long as he refuses to acknowledge the Creator, the judgment of Romans 1 is still true.

In particular – for it has educational relevance – we should note the rationalist's tendency to reduce and simplify the mysteries and complexities of the world. He needs to do it in order to achieve his dream of comprehensive knowledge. In this way he inflates human pride. Furthermore, his works involve him in a tendency to cruelty and violence. War is the dismal product of physics and easier abortion a sad culmination of modern medicine.

A CHRISTIAN ALTERNATIVE

The world shows both order and mystery, but for the rationalist they are utterly incompatible. For a Christian they are wedded. He can appreciate God's order and yet know that there is wonder and mystery in a world of which he understands so little.

Furthermore, acknowledging our sinfulness, we know that to understand the world is hard work. We do not believe that some magical system, just waiting to be discovered, will drop the secret of the whole universe in our laps. By the metaphorical sweat of our brow, we also must labour to understand. Our Christian understanding in any realm of study is very weak. Our teaching is not honest if it does not reflect that truth.

THE STYLE OF RATIONALIST EDUCATION

From the rationalist perspective, education can be made exciting. That is generally done by those who stress the thrill of man's search for the final secret of the universe. On the debit side this panders to human pride.

In actual fact, however, rationalist education is rarely made exciting. More commonly it is plain dull. It consists of the mere impartation of facts. If the teacher were to admit he himself had a struggle to understand those facts, that would be seen as an admission of intellectual incompetence. The rationalist believes and claims that there are no moral or spiritual barriers to man's grasp of the truth. If a man cannot understand the facts that others understand, then it must be because of lack of intellectual ability. Thus the teacher cannot be the model of the person who struggles and labours to understand. We have already seen that part of the humanist hope is to discover the system which will make everything easy to understand. The idea of difficulty is excluded. Thus the excitement of difficulty and accomplishment is taken away.

There is a further reason why rationalist education tends to be dull. The rationalist believes in a pot of gold at the end of the rainbow. He aims at the discovery of a final system which will make all the universe understandable and hence controllable. Certainly, order as presently understood is a stage along the way, but it is not the real goal. Thus there is a tendency to consider the immediate practical applications of what is already understood as less important than the relation of what is presently understood to the final grand scheme. For example, a physicist may scorn engineering applications of physics as compared with further research into the ultimate fundamental particle or fundamental force. Thus, in spite of the constantly reiterated plea for more practical and concrete education, rationalist teaching tends towards the theoretical. Even when the practical is combined with it, there is a gap between the theoretical and the practical. The practical will be disparaged as further from the real secret of the universe.

Like attracts like. The person who finds it relatively easy to understand complex and abstract expressions, systems, and formulae, tends to be attracted towards rationalism, and often because he enjoys showing off his ability to use complex words or expressions. The rationalist tends to think that what he believes has some approach to the final system of the universe. Hence he believes his system has the characteristics of being simple and self-evident. If people cannot understand it, that must be because of their intellectual inferiority. Such a belief is flattering to his pride. People with such convictions do not make good teachers, for they fail to see that what they find easy is difficult for others to grasp. To sympathize with a learner's difficulty in understanding, or especially to admit difficulties for oneself, would deflate pride. Further, the whole tendency to see facts as clear and cut-and-dried militates against seeing any need to explain.

When people describe the older traditional education as being dull and pedestrian, sometimes they are biased, wanting to promote something new. Yet often they have a genuine complaint for they are describing the consequences of rationalism upon education.

THE STYLE OF CHRISTIAN TEACHING

Much more needs to be considered before we can present a full picture of Christian teaching; but enough has been said for the style of Christian teaching to be set over against the style of rationalist teaching.

There is order in the world because God the Creator is its covenant Lord. That order makes knowing and doing possible. We do not deny the existence of such order out of over-reaction to rationalism. It is a Christian's aim to make a pupil's learning processes easier by helping him to perceive system and relationship in the world. However, we do not delude ourselves. No matter how much we are enabled to understand, mystery remains. There is much that we cannot understand or that we struggle to understand. The teacher must admit to this. He must realize that the pupils do not automatically understand. Hence the teacher must explain, illustrate, simplify, and repeat.

In other words the teacher must teach. One of the most persistent tendencies of non-Christian approaches to education is an ignoring of, and sometimes a strong opposition to, teaching. The rationalist will allow the 'teacher' many other roles, but that of teaching he abhors. Many will have the teacher impart facts or a method, but they completely fail to see the crucial role of the teacher as an explainer and a model.

Truth is not easy for us to grasp. If we believe what the Bible says about sin, then we must believe that truth does not come to us easily. Hence the teacher has to be the example of the one who has laboured to understand. Sympathy for those who also labour to understand will be a chief qualification for his work.

❦ 3 ❦

Romanticism and Education

THE FAILURE OF RATIONALISM

To understand romanticism, the great rival of rationalism in education, we must remember a crucial fact about the latter. Rationalism believes that there is an order and system comprehensible to the human mind which encompasses all of reality. Mystery and complexity are death blows to rationalism.

The Christian opponents of rationalism will attack it for ignoring the corruption of the human mind. Rationalism's philosophical opponents will not. They do not want to humble man! Rather they will question more whether there is really order in the universe. In that way they not only question rationalism. They question whether there is a God who rules.

For this reason the position described in the last chapter is sometimes called 'essentialism'. That is the belief that behind everything there lies an essential truth. In some ways that term is better than rationalism as it combines together rationalists in the traditional sense and empiricists. We chose the term 'rationalism' because the crucial problem is not found in the belief that there is order and truth in the creation, but in a false confidence based upon the ability of the human mind to establish all truth.

As a matter of fact the world is full of mystery. All human and rational systems are deficient at one point or another. For the rationalist a useful system is not enough. He has to have a comprehensive system. Hence rationalism is found wanting. The conclusion reached by the non-Christian is not that man is incompetent to discover the true order, but that there is no order.

It follows that what order we do perceive, man himself must have created. From that it again follows logically that education

[28]

should not be imparting facts about the order of the universe. It should be learning to create order.

The reaction against rationalism has taken place on other grounds as well. The point was made in the previous chapter that rationalism tends to attract those with particular ability in dealing with the theoretical and the abstract. What of those without such abilities? They tended to be scorned as inferior persons. Hence naturally there arose a reaction. Many felt that other aspects of man, such as imagination, emotion, and feeling, were being ignored.

Rationalism has a hope. It is a hope for the salvation of mankind. It looks forward to greater control over the universe through greater knowledge. Included in what is to be controlled is man himself. To some people that is an inviting prospect. To others it is simply frightening. Is man to be manipulated like an inanimate object? Is he to be taken apart and resynthesized like a chemical compound? Hence the revolt was partly in the name of human freedom and autonomy.

Some people see in science and its practical applications proof of the rationalist position. They picture the post-medieval period as a time of progress in health, happiness and prosperity. Others picture the same period as a slide into the ugliness of industrial towns, pollution and the destruction of the free and the beautiful. They desire a return to the rural, the primitive and the medieval. Man has lost his spirit and his freedom in the modern world.

There is a persistent tendency in Western thought in general, and in educational thought in particular, to find a link between the history of mankind and the history of the individual. People tend to see education as creating in the life of a person what has already happened in the life of the human race. Thus if you see man as progressing from barbarism and superstition through rational thought, then you will tend to see education as taking the child from ignorance to enlightenment through rational instruction. This, as we have already seen, is what rationalist education attempts to do.

Suppose you see human history as a fall from the simplicity, beauty and freedom of mankind's youth. How will you then see a child's development? You will see it as including the loss of the purity, beauty and innocence of the child.

[29]

What then should education be? Surely in this way of thinking, it must be an attempt to cling as far as possible to the stage of original innocence and freedom. There are a number of things which will threaten that innocence and freedom. Since romanticism grew as a reaction to rationalism it will reject many things associated with rationalism. That is, any ordered, systematic instruction. We must remember that such instruction must come from an adult and the adult is already seen as having lost innocence and been corrupted. Furthermore, if there is no truth or order, there is no point in systematic instruction. Such instruction tends to limit the free creativity of the child. Hence it is seen as a threat to the autonomy and freedom of the child.

Rationalism emphasizes order and system. Hence it does not emphasize individuality. It wants to understand humans as part of that system. Hence the individual differences between children are not seen as significant. Romanticism goes to the opposite extreme. It emphasizes the differences between children and is opposed to any attempt to treat them in groups.

THE TENDENCIES OF ROMANTICIST EDUCATION

Romanticist education is characterized by attempts to give maximum freedom for the development of the ability, expression and creativity of the individual child. The child is to be allowed to express himself freely. He is to be encouraged to explore for himself.

Carried to its logical extreme it would seem to imply that there is no role for a teacher except to shield the child's freedom from interfering adults. It is seldom carried to such extremes. The belief in the ability of the child to teach himself is tempered by a realization that the child must have an appropriate environment. He must have materials adjusted to his level and his individual ability. Hence romanticist education in practice is characterized more by the desire that every child should be left to work at his own individual level and left as free as possible from the controlling hand of the teacher. Thus romanticism has an antipathy to direct instruction. Instruction only makes sense if there is something true for both teacher and student. That, to a romanticist, smacks of rationalism.

Perhaps a good illustration is provided by the art teacher who was horrified by the idea that a kindergarten teacher might teach her pupils how to draw a tree. That was a threat to their free artistic creativity. It implied that there was a way in which a tree should be drawn. Rather the kindergarten teacher should allow the pupils to see and feel trees and then to draw what flowed from their own perception and experience of a tree. In the terms of the earlier discussion, he was not so radical as to expect children to make their own paints. He did however expect them to paint without any direct instruction in the techniques of art.

THE ROMANTICIST HOPE

We have seen that the rationalist is very much inspired by a hope for the salvation of mankind. The romanticist also has a hope. It lies in a generation who will be able to preserve the purity and creativity of childhood and come to adult leadership without the corrupting influences handed down from former generations. They will then be able to solve the world's problems.

The school once more plays a vital role in this hope. For it is in school that innocence and creativity are to be protected and nurtured. Romanticist teachers commonly see the home, with its discipline and its passing on of attitudes and beliefs, as their major enemy.

THE FUNDAMENTAL ERROR OF ROMANTICISM

Whatever we may think about this or that aspect of romanticist education, there is a fundamental error rooted in what is believed about the child. It is certainly true that bad example, bad company and bad teaching will have a corrupting influence on a child. That, however, does not prove that the child begins life in complete innocency. The Scripture clearly teaches original corruption (Psalms 51:5; 58:3; Genesis 8:21; Proverbs 22:15; Ephesians 2:3).

It may be argued that this is a moral or spiritual corruption, and as such is not relevant to education. However, there is an obvious relationship between the child's character and his ability to receive education. First, it must be insisted that the fact of original sin in the child destroys the romanticist hope. There is corruption in the heart and mind as well as in the adult environment around the child. Free expression and development, be it little or plentiful, is quite unable to deal with the internal problem.

Further, the internal character of the child has significance for the education process. This significance is often overlooked because of a measure of truth in one of romanticism's doctrines, namely, that of individuality. There is a difference between children. Some children do have an element of academic self-motivation. How much that is due to inherited character and how much it is due to home influences is really not relevant. The fact is that it is present. Children in this category may show their depravity in some other way; for example, in displaying pride or stubbornness. The romanticist points to such children and claims that they reveal the true nature of all children who will teach themselves if only given the opportunity. Denying his own doctrine of individuality, he fails to consider the other children whose besetting sin may be laziness. Of course the romanticist system can come up with all sorts of other explanations for the lazy child's failure to achieve success in a romanticist school. The home can always be blamed!

This is not to suggest that the child who does well academically out of pride and desire for prominence, has no educational problems. Indeed his major problem may well be the very thing that romanticists treasure most. He may lack original thought!

Children are very good at catching the indirect clues which teachers and adults give of what they expect. In spite of romanticist doctrine it is natural for a child to seek to do what his teachers desire. Often children who are mentally alert will detect the clues that teachers give. They then receive the praise and status which such achievement gives. The romanticist teacher fondly believes that here are children doing what the doctrine requires. They are acting as children are 'supposed' to act. In reality they may be conforming simply to what is expected in their school. Conformity, in romanticist doctrine, is the very opposite of originality.

There are also students who fail to do what the doctrine requires. They do not show inventiveness and originality. What happens to them in such a system? Either the teacher forgets the dogma and teaches them, or they do not learn and are the victims of the dogma.

DISCIPLINE

For many the mention of discipline within a school context immediately raises the issue of corporal punishment. That is not the crucial issue. The crucial issue is whether the child needs restraint in one form or another as well as encouragement. Anybody truly converted to romanticism will deny the need for restraint. For restraint comes from the adult community which is seen as repressive. To admit the need of restraint is to admit that the child is not originally good. Of course practical necessity often triumphs over dogma and some form of discipline is used.

Proverbs is a biblical book which has much to say on the raising of children. Many times it brings together the child's depravity and the need for discipline and training. Proverbs 22:15 has already been mentioned: 'Foolishness is bound up in the heart of a child; The rod of discipline will remove it far from him.' Similar thoughts are found in Proverbs 13:24 and 23:13, 14.

This part of the biblical teaching cannot be used to set aside biblical teaching which stresses the need for encouragement, example and affection in our relation to all men, and especially to children. Nevertheless we see in Proverbs that its teaching on the training of children fits practice to the nature of the child. Romanticism attempts to do this. It shapes its educational method according to its mistaken belief in the goodness and original innocence of the child. Christians must make their practice conform with their belief in original sin.

THE PRAGMATIC JUSTIFICATION OF ROMANTICISM

One rarely meets with a true and consistent romanticism. The free school in which every child is allowed to do as he likes soon collapses, but it is quite common to find schools where attempts are made to incorporate some elements of romanticism into education without adopting the extreme form. People who do this cannot give a philosophical defence of what they are doing, for to adopt pure romanticism would mean they had to adopt its practical failure. They are in the dilemma of liking romanticism but knowing that it cannot work in its abstract form.

Hence they will attempt to justify aspects of educational practice of romanticist origin on pragmatic grounds. It is claimed that we grasp better and retain better what we have had to work out for ourselves. In defence of every child proceeding at his own pace, it is argued that this makes due allowance for the individual differences between children.

a) *Self-teaching*

The claim that a child understands best what he works out for himself may be quite true or quite false. It may be based upon unfair comparisons. It may be founded on recollections of school which prove something entirely different.

For example, suppose that a school possesses a very poor teacher. His explanations are muddled and confusing. As a result a learner cannot do the work until in desperation he sits down and works out an understanding for himself. Such an experience might leave him with the conviction that he understands best what he does for himself. Yet had the teacher been a good teacher, teaching something a child had once tried to do but failed, then his impressions might be quite different. Often we spend more time on what we work out for ourselves than on what we are taught. That in itself might explain a greater impact. Yet there are only so many hours in a day. We cannot learn everything for ourselves from first principles, even if we are capable of doing so.

There are several biblical teachings which relate to this discussion. Scripture is emphatic that there are things which it is better not to learn from experience. One of these is the pain of doing things the wrong way. This is one of the themes of the early chapters of Proverbs. The youth who listens to the instruction of the wise will not need to experience the remorse that follows sin (see especially 5:11–14). There are things that we should not learn by experience, but rather accept via instruction.

Scripture also makes it clear that true knowledge does not exist in a vacuum. It must be accompanied by obedience. We learn the truth in order that we may respond to it in deeds of obedient love. Knowledge is not separated from life in some theoretical and impractical realm. Hence we should have a concern for pupils to be able to turn knowledge into action. That does not mean that we should learn only by doing. It does mean that learning and doing should not be kept separate.

Hence we cannot make any iron-clad rules about experience being always the best way to learn things. We can say that knowledge and practical experience need to be kept in the right relationship. The decision on whether we want pupils to teach themselves will depend on other factors.

b) *Individual Ability and Curriculum Objectives*

How much material should a child cover in a particular grade? That question produces very different answers. Some would even regard it as illegitimate. The rationalist can answer the question because he holds there is an objective body of truth to be mastered by the pupil. Hence that can be broken down into material to be learned in various grades. The romanticist will reject the question. He denies that there is such a body of truth and he would have each child set his own agenda for learning.

How should the Christian respond to the problem? The point has already been made that knowledge should be connected to acts of obedience. The Scripture says much about Christian growth. The growth is a growth in knowledge but it is also a growth in resultant obedience (e.g. Ephesians 3:16–19; 4:13–16; Philippians 4:8, 9; Hebrews 5:11–14). Such is the growth we also desire for our children.

Some educationalists may object that we should not bring in adult goals when we think of children's education. It will be objected that we then fall into the trap of treating children as 'little adults' instead of recognizing their distinctive character as children.

This objection is easily answered. Children have to grow up and they should grow up. Scripture sees the state of childhood, not as a state to long for and hold on to, but as a state to grow out of (Hebrews 5:13, 14; Ephesians 4:14). The problem arises if we regard children as starting as adults, rather than recognizing the problems and difficulties they encounter as children. We must realize where they begin, but never lose sight of the end that is in view.

To return to the main point, there is a goal for which we aim. It is functioning Christian maturity. The school is certainly not alone in working to reach that goal. It works to supplement the home, and the home works together with the church. We could think of many things which are part of Christian maturity but let us restrict the discussion to the things that particularly concern the school.

Excluding cases of physical disability, we would expect to find the following abilities in a mature adult: the ability to read, to understand what is read, and to communicate it to others; the ability to earn a living and provide for one's family; a knowledge of

[35]

the history of God's people and of the struggle of the church against the world; some understanding of the whole world as it relates to the missionary task of the church; the ability to instruct one's own children in these things; some knowledge of the world God has made and appreciation of its wonder; some ability to provide for the physical need of food and clothing; such musical knowledge and/or skill as will facilitate the praise of God; appreciation of and, hopefully, some skill in reflecting the beauty of God's creation in our own works. For a child with a particular gift or aim we might hope for much more. This is a minimal list.

There is nothing here which might not reasonably be expected of a mature Christian. As parents we desire that our children attain to such maturity. The school is an aid to such growth. There are things on this list which are connected with spiritual sensitivity and perception. Our children will not attain to them without the work of the Spirit of God in them. There are other things which consist of knowledge and skills which can in some measure be learned by an unbeliever. An unbeliever can learn to write, though he will not use it for the same purpose. The school cannot set curriculum goals in terms of things which require the Holy Spirit's enlightenment. It does not control the Spirit. It can reasonably set goals in terms of those things which may be learned, in some measure, without the Spirit's help. In doing so it does nothing different from what a parent does. A Christian parent requires his children to be obedient and respectful. He cannot say 'I will require nothing of them until they are converted by the Spirit of God', for this would involve him in finding an excuse for not doing what the Bible tells him to do. The fact that we cannot control God is no excuse for failing to obey God's commands. Similarly the school, acting to help parents guide their children to Christian maturity, cannot refuse to teach on the ground that proper use of this knowledge requires the work of the Spirit of God. The school has a goal to reach and it plans, under God, to reach that goal.

That goal in turn gives content and pace to the curriculum. If there is a certain amount to be achieved at the end of schooling, then it is logical to break that down into amounts appropriate to the child's ability at a particular age.

Thus we have seen that the claim that we learn best if we teach ourselves cannot be accepted without reservation. We have also seen that the school has a goal in mind in its instruction and may reasonably divide the progress towards that goal into graded steps. We have also seen that knowledge and practice may not be separated.

It would be an injustice to romanticism to imply that the romanticist's education does not have a goal. They too aim at maturity of character and ability, but independence from law and restraint is very much a part of their definition of maturity. They insist, in a way correctly, that the means of education must be consistent with the goal of education. If the goal is creativity and independence then the means cannot be a method which does not allow the child independence.

Similarly the Christian approach relates means and ends. Our goal is a person who has internalized the law and standards of God. He is self-disciplined so that he can devote his energies and give his attention not to himself alone, but also to meeting the needs of others. Hence, law and discipline are part of the means to that end.

Another way of putting the same point is to draw attention to the fact that romanticist education assumes that a good measure of maturity already exists in the child. The child wants to teach himself and has at least some of the skills for doing so. Christian education does not assume ideal starting conditions. It is adapted to work with children who may not be self-motivated. It can do this because it combines together specific instruction, encouragement, and discipline. That is to say, it begins by telling the child specifically what he is to do. It tells him why, as a creature of God, preparing to serve God, he should learn. It warns him of the discipline that will follow failure to obey.

If a child is already self-motivated to learn, if he is already 'adult', then it will not permanently warp his personality for him to have that desire to learn reinforced. The superiority of Christian education really becomes clear when it comes to the child without the initial motivation or skills. Such a child suffers in the romanticist system.

While it is not a necessary part of the romanticist system, many teachers influenced by this doctrine resort at this point to the idea of individual differences. They are much interested in tests like I.Q. tests, for the failure of many children to learn in such a system can then be blamed on their lack of initial ability. Obviously, there are all sorts of problems with such tests. They do not merely detect inherent ability. They are influenced by cultural factors and training. Much more serious is the creation of self-fulfilling prophecy. A child who is judged as being of low ability is given little encouragement and help to achieve.

If, however, for argument's sake, we concede that such tests are accurate, what should we do with the pupil who has less inherent ability and motivation? Should we place such children in a system which assumes the initial ability? Is it not more loving and more realistic to take them through small steps of direct instruction and encouragement in order to build those skills?

Some methods attempt to arrange the child's environment so that the child's self-teaching from the environment progresses in small manageable steps. Such methods work to a degree where the child is able and the home has already taught good habits. It is where starting conditions are not ideal that the problems of romanticist assumptions about children become more obvious.

We must make it clear that our desire is not that the child remain permanently dependent upon such specific help. Our desire is that the child may reach the maturity of being motivated by his own knowledge of God's truth. On the other hand, we want to escape the dilemma which is currently troubling education systems. We have 'experts' who are oriented in thinking and experience more towards secondary or even tertiary pupils. They devise infant and primary curricula which assume very mature attitudes and skills on the part of young children. A large number of children do not learn in such a system. They arrive at high school or college poorly equipped. Their future teachers are not then in a position to institute courses which involve considerable individual initiative. Thus the child, having been asked to teach himself before he was ready for it, is later not in a position to take more responsibility for his own learning.

Thus our objection to the idea that every child be left to teach himself, is not an objection of absolute principle. It is rather a recognition of the fact that the child is not an adult. He does not yet have the needed maturity to decide what should be learned. He may lack the internal self-discipline. He may need to be taught a variety of skills and essential truths.

The consequence of allowing each child to proceed at the pace he himself sets is that the goal that the school has set may not be reached. The child who is not self-motivated will be left behind. If the school allows that to happen, then the child who comes to school with the greater problems is penalized by the system. That is not consistent with fairness or charity.

THE 'GIFTED' CHILD

The claim that children should be allowed to proceed at their own pace is generally made on behalf of the 'gifted' child, that is to say, the child who tends to do well in the things that schools are able to teach and to test. It can be argued that in his case it is tolerably certain that he will reach the desired curriculum objectives, although his attempts to reach his true potential may be hampered by the need to wait for the rest of the class to catch him up!

This issue is an emotive one, for some parents feel strongly that their child is being denied the opportunity he should receive. It may be a major factor in their transferring a child to a Christian school.

At this point it needs to be pointed out that teachers seldom face an absolute alternative where the choice has to be made between a 'gifted' child's achieving his potential and a co-ordinated school curriculum. However, let us assume for the sake of the argument that such is the case. Let us assume a clear and absolute choice. The school may adopt a policy of each child proceeding at his own pace. The consequence will be that the more academically able will do very well but the less able may suffer severely. If learning 'at his own pace' must be faster for the 'gifted' child, then, in the absence of outside influence, it must be slower for the academically weaker child. Alternatively the school may choose to hold the class to a curriculum. The result will be that the able do not progress as far, but the less able are not left as far behind.

If a choice has to be made between these alternatives, for the Christian there can be only one choice. The gospel requires compassion towards the poor and the needy. It is not biased towards the successful and the gifted. We cannot put our further advancement, when we are already successful, ahead of the needs of the person who is failing.

Let it be stressed that this choice is proposed only for the sake of the argument. In everyday life the choice is normally much less clear. There are many ways in which the academically gifted child

[39]

benefits from direct instruction instead of being allowed to work everything out for himself. Many good students can work out their own course of action without really understanding the full ramifications of the subject.

So far the discussion has assumed that certain children really are exceptional. Yet it is a sad fact that many supposedly 'gifted' ones are average children through whom parents live out their own ambitions. Such children have enough problems without being left to do everything for themselves. Very few students excel in all areas of school work. They may do so in more theoretical subjects, but may lack competence when it comes to the requirements of manual dexterity. They may be good at mathematics but poor at English, or vice versa. What naturally happens when such a child is left to teach himself is that he will concentrate on the things he finds easy. An organized curriculum makes the child work at, and develop competence in, tasks that are not easily accomplished. Growth in maturity is thus stimulated.

Closely related to this whole question is that of homogeneous grouping. That is to say, do we attempt to separate children into groups which are alike in ability or do we mix the ability groups? It is very hard to get clear evidence of which is best from an educational point of view. That is because other factors, for example, the quality of the teaching, have such a crucial influence on the results. Both the official studies and the impressions of a number of teachers can be interpreted as leading to the conclusion that able students do better in homogeneous grouping and less able students do worse. The reasons for this result are fairly obvious. A class that is uniformly able can move through the material much more quickly. However, if a group of pupils is brought together, all of whom have problems, then there is no pupil to act as an example and an incentive to other pupils. The class settles down to a uniform mediocrity.

Most of our Christian schools are small. They do not give much opportunity to separate pupils into classes of greater and lesser ability. If the conclusion is correct that the more able pupils do not progress so quickly in the heterogeneous classes which must result, should the parents of these more able pupils avoid Christian schools?

That brings us back to a question which has already been considered. For while the able child might lose something academically, he does serve as an example and encouragement to others. Surely Christian principle leads us to say that the Christian parent of an able child should place the child in a Christian school.

So far, however, our discussion has omitted consideration of many important factors. A student in a heterogeneous Christian school may do much better academically than in the homogeneous alternative. That will happen just because the Christian school is academically better. Even when it does not work out this way there are other factors to be considered. The child is receiving a *Christian* education. That is a factor of the first importance. Many good pupils are hampered by a lack of ability to relate to other people. They can immerse themselves in their books and achieve good results, but they have problems with their slower fellows. For such a child, learning to wait while a poorer student struggles is one of the most important parts of his education. We are not interested in bright graduates without love. The Christian school aims at real Christian maturity.

Much of what has been said thus far will perhaps leave the impression that the able pupil is penalized academically by attending a Christian school. The real truth is that, even *if* this happens, there are a variety of compensations. Whether it does happen depends upon the quality of the teaching. Only a good teacher can deal with the great range of ability one finds in Christian schools. But the fact is well established, that the child who is able, who is well taught and not allowed just to muddle through with native intuition, who is made to work even at what he finds more difficult, and who works within a controlled and disciplined class, that child is not going to come out worse in the end. He may not be doing eighth-grade mathematics while in fifth grade. On the other hand his attitude to others and his handwriting while in eighth grade may not be inferior to that of a fifth grader.

THE CHILD WITH DISABILITIES

A strong case can be made out for allowing a child to proceed at his own pace when he has disabilities. Obviously in cases of very severe mental or physical disability, the expectation of success cannot be equal to that of an average child. That point is simply not disputable. However, there are some important clarifications and qualifications to be made. It is still important for the disabled child's education to have a goal and to make some progress. If an unrealistic goal is not a help neither is the absence of a goal. The child needs to be set aims he can reach, and thus grow.

In particular he needs to grow in self-discipline. The handicapped child has enough problems without having to contend with his own lack of discipline. It is false kindness to expect nothing of a handicapped child. The knowledge of how much to expect requires wisdom, patience and experience.

Other pupils will confront us with a different set of problems. Their poor performance in school work cannot be traced to any obvious physical cause. Numerous questions arise: should they be put in with a normal class? should they be expected to do the same work as others?

Some pupils of this type will respond to a system in which each child works at his own pace. That is because there is no longer the constant reminder of failure, as compared to the achievement of the rest of the class. That may postpone the moment of 'failure'. Most school systems have some measure of successful completion at the end of the course, some graduation certificate, diploma, etc. A child who does not receive such certification because of physical disability may be disappointed but he has no sense of failure if he has done the best of which he is capable. The situation is difficult for the child with no such obvious disability. He may escape the daily feeling of failure and yet emerge at the end, because he did not complete school, with a crushing sense of failure. Yet there may be some real but undiagnosed physical problem which explains his poor performance.

In this whole matter there are no easy answers. There is only a need for great wisdom and sensitivity. What we teach in school is important both for the child's sense of accomplishment and for the child's service to God. If we can find a way of enabling the child to do the work with some measure of success, then let us work at it. School experience teaches the importance of the obvious, yet the overlooked. Some children labelled as poor readers simply need glasses.

Certain factors that are fashionable in current educational practices make things difficult for the slower child. In particular the hostility to direct teaching that comes from romanticism is a problem. Since the slower child finds it harder to work things out for himself, he needs direct teaching that is clear, vivid, and above all, repeated. Here is where the school must function as a community. If parents are available to devote individual time to the child's needs, to clarify and to reinforce the points taught, so much the better!

If there is a teacher especially trained to work with such children, then that is a real bonus. Yet we must realize that the money for employing such teachers is short in many Christian schools. Many schools will have to do the best they can without such extra help. It is a mark of the success of Christian schools that parents of handicapped children are turning in numbers to the Christian school rather than to the state systems, which do have many more facilities and often the specialized personnel, for such problems. Christian schools may bemoan their lack of resources but often they are doing better than those with resources.

One outstanding reason for this relative success is undoubtedly the love and encouragement found in the Christian school community. The problem of the discouragement a student has with failure was mentioned earlier. The love and encouragement of the teacher, of parents, and of fellow pupils are important means of overcoming a child's troubled feelings. Here the rationalist who delights in his theorizing has nothing to offer. The romanticist who wishes the child to be left alone to express himself can give no help. The child needs the support of others as he faces what is to him a very great and difficult challenge. There are few teaching techniques as effective as love.

Rationalism makes the prized and esteemed student to be the one with analytic and rational gifts. In reaction to this, romanticism has become almost anti-intellectual. It has tended to value the pupil with artistic gifts or gifts of expression. We may see such gifts as gifts from God and appreciate them. Yet the person who has these gifts is not necessarily great in the kingdom of God. The blessings of that kingdom are to the obedient. Thus a child needs to be reminded that his struggles in school, by comparison with those who seem to find the work easy, say nothing about the way God views him. Sometimes the assurance that God's eye is upon him is all that is needed to take away the fear of failure and to encourage him to succeed.

There may be times when none of these methods and efforts seem to produce good results. We hesitate to pressure the child to further effort for fear we lay a cruel burden on one who is doing the best he can with a disability we do not understand. Yet with another child whose performance is equivalent we may strongly suspect that the problem is behavioural. Sometimes lack of co-operation from the home in dealing with the problem is a factor. In cases like this we may simply have to alter what we expect of the child and pray for greater wisdom.

ROMANTICISM AND ANALYSIS

Rationalism depends upon a commitment to analysis, namely, to the breaking of problems and things down into simpler components which can then be more easily understood and controlled. Romanticism tends to reject that as cold, mechanical and unfeeling. If man is analysed as nothing but a bag of chemicals, then of what worth is man? If our experiences and feelings are analysed as a set of conditioned reflexes, then they seem to be cheapened. For romanticism, to analyse is to destroy. Situations have to be experienced in their wholeness.

This romanticist conviction has very important implications for teaching. It means that the teacher should not be breaking instruction down into pieces digestible by the student. He should be giving the student experiences in their entirety. In practice there is a problem here. If there is no way to pick out the significant in the experience, then the pupil is confronted with a bewildering mass of experiences. The following illustration will help to explain the problem.

Let us suppose we found ourselves in a foreign country whose language we could not understand. At first we would believe that all its people talked at a very fast rate, so much so that we could not distinguish one word from another. Given long enough, however, we would come to understand the language. Eventually we would recognize the patterns and repetitions. We would connect words to situations and eventually learn what at first completely puzzled us. A person with particular aptitude for languages would naturally perceive those relationships more quickly.

Alternatively, suppose a native was to break the language up for us. For our sakes he spoke it slowly and distinctly. He explained its structure and analysed it for us, alerting us to listen for certain constructions. Undoubtedly we would then learn the language more easily and quickly.

Romanticism has a strong bias towards the first of these alternatives, not necessarily in language learning only, but in all learning. The child is to experience the fullness of the phenomena and to train himself to discover instinctively the various patterns and relationships. They should not be pointed out to him.

The practical problem can be guessed from the illustration about language. Some children have particular aptitude in seeing such relationships. They may not learn as fast as when the relationships are pointed out to them. But they definitely learn. Others have far greater trouble. They fail to discover the patterns and relationships and as a result fall behind the others academically. That failure is not blamed on the teaching method but on their I.Q.

As Christians we do not have such problems with analysis. Something like a language has order and structure. Hence it can be analysed. We can point out those regularities. However it cannot all be reduced to a system. You cannot start with a set of first principles and deduce all the grammatical structures of English or any other language. In learning any language a certain amount of patience, hard work and memorization is indispensable.

The structure and order and yet the variety and ultimate unpredictability of language should not be surprising. For it is part of the creation.

This opposition to analysis has other manifestations as well. The breaking of the curriculum into subject areas is a form of analysis. Romanticists are generally opposed to it for that reason. Often the reason given is that such teaching fragments the child's education. He receives bits of knowledge but not knowledge connected and related. It is argued that we should present not abstract subjects but concrete things out of the child's world and experience. These things can be explored for their different aspects and connections. The thing or theme chosen gives a coherence to the child's learning. What is important is that the thing be viewed in its wholeness: in all its wide variety of ramifications.

This position produces problems for the Christian school, which, as we have seen, has a limited role. It does not seek to cover all of life because it supplements the home which is already covering much of the territory. That does not mean that its approach lacks unity. Its approach is unified by commitment to biblical principles. But the area in which it operates is a restricted one.

Further, the Christian school has certain goals, as we have seen. It could build its curriculum by investigating every aspect of life or institution in the child's experience. That is usually so large, however, as to be impractical. It has to choose. What is to guide the choice? If it chooses its curriculum in order to be assured that, say, by Grade 8 or 9 this topic has been covered in geography and that in history, then it has chosen its approach. The thing really structuring the curriculum is the subject history and the subject geography and the reaching of certain goals in these subjects. The true romanticist would maintain that there is no goal other than the expanding of the child's world of experience. Any aim of covering so much by such a time assumes an objective content outside the child. That is anathema to the romanticist.

Many schools try to combine both approaches. Instead of material organized to build a particular discipline, they have a series of units based upon something in the child's world. But they are constantly looking over their shoulder, as it were, to try to make sure the child learns a certain amount in crucial areas.

For Christians, man's experience, and the child's experience in particular, are not the educational standard. We do not have to organize our curriculum around that. If we do, we face a major problem of disunity. If a child is taught in terms of units organized around a variety of things drawn from the child's experience, what provides the unity between the material learned in the various units? The true romanticist is not troubled by this question because the unity in the child's experience is all-important to him. But the person who is trying to teach history and science and mathematics by this indirect route has a major problem. How is the history taught in one unit to be connected with the history taught through another? If the units are chosen so that there is a continuity in the history, what happens to the science?

This is not to be construed as a defence of traditional subject boundaries. There is a unity in creation which is often obscured by the way subjects are divided. We can organize the material some other way. For example does instruction in the requirements of health naturally belong with physical education or with science? Should we cut the common connection of geography and history and develop a unified course connecting geography more with the sciences? All such rethinking is quite legitimate. The important thing is that the structure of the curriculum is determined by the goal and not by the world of experience of the supposedly autonomous child.

It makes much more sense to develop a coherent curriculum to reach the desired goal, say in history or mathematics, rather than to hope that a unified grasp of history and mathematics will somehow emerge from units on the local senior citizens centre, the local council, what the class had for breakfast, etc. That is not to say the class can never consider the senior citizens centre. However, that consideration should be integrated into the school's ultimate curriculum goal.

The common objection to this is that the child is really interested only in the world of his own experience. That will be considered in the next chapter.

∾ 4 ∾

The Social Role of the School

The previous two chapters talked about two major influences on education. Perhaps we should have talked about three, the third being the emphasis on the social role of the school that is generally connected with the name of John Dewey. Just as rationalism and romanticism have been modified and changed, so Dewey's ideas and those of others of similar tendencies, have been popularized and adapted.

The popularized form has come through in an insistence that pupils work co-operatively rather than individually, also in a tendency to see social adaptation as one of the prime roles of the school.

THE RECAPITULATION HERESY

One of the most powerful influences in education this century is an idea that biologists consider to be a disproved theory, namely, the theory of recapitulation. In its biological form it is the theory that the embryo during development repeats stages of evolution through which the organism has passed. As a biological theory it has long since been disproved and discarded. In other disciplines it is still a pervasive image and idea. One could cite, for example, the idea that 'backward races' are still in the 'childhood' of the human race.

In education the dominant expression of this picture has been the belief that the child has to learn and develop in the same way that man evolved as an animal. It is asserted that man evolved by an active interaction with his environment. Man, or his pre-human precursor, had to struggle for existence within the environment. Out of that struggle came change and development. So the child

[48]

has to experience tensions in interaction with the environment in order to come to discoveries which resolve and overcome those tensions.

While different from Dewey in many ways, the same commitment to the evolutionary analogy occurs in Piaget's theories. One of the consequences of taking this analogy between evolution and education seriously is an opposition to direct instruction. That is because direct instruction changes the child without the child having to struggle with the environment. If one continues working with the parallel to the history of the human race, then the counterpart to direct instruction in the history of man would be special creation. It is probably significant that the Bible teaches both that God created man and that the father is to instruct the child. In biblical perspective man is not an autonomous creature who shapes himself by interaction with his environment. He is created and shaped.

The educational consequence of this evolutionary analogy is a dedication to learning by interaction. The child must explore and discover for himself. He must meet tensions and problems and learn to overcome them.

RECREATING SOCIAL HARMONY

A second major concern of Dewey was what he saw as the loss of social harmony and consensus. Part of that loss was caused by urbanization and industrialization. The close-knit community of the village is no more. More significant is the belief that the old religious and moral basis of the community is viable no longer. In other words, Dewey's antagonism to Christianity plays a major role in his thought at this point. For him Christianity has been disproved by science. He was consistent enough to see that you could not reject the doctrine of Christianity and retain its morality. Doctrine and morality live or die together.

Hence there was a need to discover a new moral basis for the community. How could this be done? Dewey saw the method of science as the answer. Science explores, evaluates and discovers. So we must explore and test to find a new morality. The school was to be the place where men learned how to do this. Since the crucial thing was to discover a new foundation for the community, the search had to be a communal search. The school was to be the place where people learned how to co-operate together in order to reach common objectives. Here is another instance of the way in which the goal of learning must influence the method of learning. If the goal is social cohesion then education cannot be individualistic. Children have to learn as an interacting social unit.

When we put this together with the previous section, we can see the form education must take. It has to be an exploratory interaction with the environment during which tensions arise or problems emerge which the group as a whole learns to overcome. Success is achieved only by the finding of something which works.

THE POLITICAL CHILD

In Dewey's writings and speeches the idea of democracy occurs repeatedly. His ideal was a secular, humanist democracy in which men worked together to overcome their problems. Of course there is a major question. Do men really want to do that? The question can also be asked about the child. Does the child really want to be a communal problem solver? Essentially Dewey was convinced that he did. The child was seen as intrinsically active and inquisitive, as one concerned about his immediate environment and its tensions and problems. Thus the child is interested in history or myth only for their relevance to the existing situation. Thus Dewey recasts the child in his own image. Since the solution of the problems of present society are Dewey's major concern, so they must be the child's major concern.

To admit that the child had any other sort of interest in the past, or in fantasy, would be to destroy the whole endeavour. The child is not being deliberately taught to be a solver of communal problems. If Christianity is untrue there is no basis for urging a child to be a peace-maker and to do good to his neighbour. Hence one must start with the premise that the child is vitally interested in his immediate environment and wants to solve its problems. If he is not, then the whole endeavour collapses.

If the child is so vitally interested in his present environment and in other things only as they relate to it, then it makes sense to direct education to those interests. Hence the conviction that education must focus on the world of the child's experience. Sometimes adapters of the Dewey method will attempt to start from the child's immediate world and expand his horizons somewhat. Yet the fundamental conviction that the child is not interested in those distant horizons puts a damper on such attempts.

One of the consequences of these ideas has been a strong aversion to history. The world's geography, as opposed to local geography, has also suffered. This must be a concern to Christians because Christianity is rooted in the events of past history and has a global perspective. That is not to say that, to begin with, the child should aim to attain to a historical and geographical perspective of global proportions. Nevertheless the Christian sees it as a vital concern to expand the horizons. When one does so then one discovers an interesting fact. Children love stories about the strange and the different. In the same way that the small child who cannot walk far loves to be taken to see what is outside the range of his short legs, so the child wants his world to be expanded. Dewey notwithstanding, children naturally grow by absorbing what others tell them. They are not intrinsically autonomous humanists who are dedicated to working their own world out for themselves. Given their sinful and selfish inclinations they may become concerned only for themselves if we do not expand their horizons.

RATIONALISM, ROMANTICISM, AND DEWEY

One can take elements of this position and combine it either with rationalism or with romanticism.

Dewey had elements of rationalism in his belief in a rational social morality which man could discover for himself. Hence the discovery method which he fostered can be interpreted rationalistically. It can be seen as the search for order. Yet the method also can be adapted to romanticism. The child is not taught, but discovers things for himself; or rather, he decides for himself what solution is appropriate for himself.

There has been something of a shift towards the latter interpretation. Dewey was, after all, a believer in an absolute moral system. He had not found it in its entirety but he believed it could be found. In an age of relativism such absolutes are not popular. Dewey could advocate studying another society to learn things which could help us in our own society. A relativist studies other societies only to learn that other societies differ in values and there are no absolutes. Otherwise stated, we could claim that Dewey sought a morality that would bind whole communities together. But our age has decided that there can be no such morality. Each man must be his own law.

The result is that the method of education remains but it has lost what original purpose it had.

THE DEGENERATION OF THE METHOD

Hence what we encounter today is a degenerate form of the Dewey method. The conviction may continue that there is something magical about children working in groups. Hence they will be seated around a table. Yet the teacher will give a certain amount of direct instruction, causing pain to the child who has to twist around from his place at the table to see the teacher, or to look at what he is writing on the board. Most school work may take the form of projects which children are supposed to work on together, but the school is still caught in a system where employers or tertiary institutions want to select individual students rather than the whole class. The group discovery method has lost its original purpose and justification. Yet it continues. Probably its continuance arises out of educators' awareness that Dewey was correct on one point. If you take away Christianity, men will find it difficult to live together.

SOCIAL HARMONY: THE CHRISTIAN RESPONSE

We agree with Dewey that there is a problem in making people live in harmony. Dewey believed that autonomous man had to use the methods of science to discover the solution to that problem. He did not believe that the solution had been revealed to man in the law of God. Perhaps this contrast will make the approach to these problems found in the Book of Proverbs easier to understand. Proverbs is also concerned about social morality. The young man is to learn it by listening to those made wise by the law of God. Similarly the New Testament Epistles instruct us how we are to relate to one another.

Yet we must remember also that this knowledge is to be put into practice. As James and 1 John emphasize, it must be demonstrated in Christian lives in this 'present evil world'.

How does this relate to the training of children? As Christian parents we instruct our offspring in what is right in their relationship with others and we require them to practise it. In one sense that does require a kind of social situation. An only child can appear sweet and well behaved until he is confronted with the experience of having to share his toys with other children. Parents of an only child might well take steps to ensure that the child is required to put into practice their teaching on sharing. However it is not the experience of playing with children, as such, that makes the child share. The problem is to bring his selfish nature under control. An only child who has been taught and disciplined by Christian parents will make much more progress towards that end than an undisciplined child from a large family.

What part does the Christian school play in this matter? It upholds the standards that have been taught in the home. Thus it will require a standard of kind behaviour and mutual concern in its pupils. In applying Christian principles to the whole of life it might well enter into a consideration of the relevance of those principles in political circles or in the situation depicted in some work of literature. Yet one cannot say that it has a major role in discovering those principles. The main problem is not the discovering of the principles, but the personal unwillingness of sinful men to apply them.

THE PRAGMATIC JUSTIFICATION OF GROUP LEARNING

As Dewey's ideas have filtered down to teachers, some of whom are not aware of his premises and goals, they have undergone a common transformation. Instead of being defended as the ideas needed to save a secular democratic society, they are defended as producing better educational practice. It will be claimed that children learn better this way since they can learn from each other in group projects.

This assertion is made so frequently that society at large might suppose that it must be true. One can agree in the sense that children who work well do serve as models to other children. Example, good or bad, starts working as a factor very early in life. Yet children do not necessarily have to work in group projects in order to be aware of the standard and example set by other children.

[53]

Yet there is a problem with group work. It is that some students work and some do not. Once again it is interesting to consider the teaching of the Book of Proverbs: 'He who walks with wise men will be wise, but the companion of fools will suffer harm' (13:20). We do learn from one another. The most profit, however, is to be obtained from association with those who have something to teach. A good and conscientious pupil in a group working together may stimulate others to work and correct their inclination to discouragement or laziness. Yet it is the rae child who can overcome a serious problem in another child. That generally requires adult maturity. More often what happens is that the conscientious child does all the work and the others are confirmed in their sense of inadequacy or their laziness.

There are real problems when this commitment to group work is combined with romanticism, for then there is a strong bias against the teacher having any real instructive role. The trained and mature person from whom pupils need to learn is barred from instructing them.

Obviously there are tasks in which children have to work together. Commonly, pupils who work together best are those who have learned two lessons. The one is the biblical teaching on love and sharing mentioned earlier. The other is to become a responsible worker who can be entrusted with part of the task and will complete it. For this latter quality to come to maturity a child has to learn to execute tasks. He cannot rely upon others to do them. That means he must be given tasks he himself must carry out.

There is another problem with the group learning model that flows from the goal of the school discussed earlier. Our aim is to contribute to the growth in maturity of each child. There is a standard that each child must reach. It is not sufficient that the co-operating group achieves it by its co-operative efforts. Each child must reach it.

Of course many teachers who implement the group learning model are simply following what was taught them in whatever education courses they followed. Yet they do so against their instincts as teachers. Thus you have the marriage of incompatibilities. Children are permanently seated in groups facing each other around tables. Yet the teacher tries to focus their attention on him and on the blackboard. Naturally the child, whose back is permanently to the teacher, finds it easier to concentrate on the child across the table than on the teacher.

If it is true that nobody has more truth than anybody else; if it is true that we must search together for the truth; if it is true that the uncorrupted child will be a better teacher than an adult; then let us arrange our classrooms accordingly. If it is true that the teacher, who has absorbed and applied the Word of God to himself and his subjects, is wiser than the pupils, then let us arrange the classroom accordingly.

THE CHRISTIAN SCHOOL AND SOCIAL ADAPTATION

One way in which this emphasis on the social role of the school has influenced people, has been in seeing the school as the major way people learn to relate in social situations. Social adaptation is considered a major role of the school. In some circles this has been turned into another religious hope. If we can only put the children of the conflicting groups in society together, then we will have peace in society in the next generation. People who have such a belief are generally very antagonistic to the Christian school. In it they see one group withdrawing its children from this socializing process in the state schools.

People who hold such a hope subscribe to a form of the common view which sees hatred as a result of ignorance. If people only knew each other better, then there would be no hatred. Jesus teaches to the contrary. The evils which disfigure human life come from the human heart (Mark 7:20–23). Merely bringing people together will do nothing to solve this. Rather, the great cities where men are brought together are the places in which sin breeds vanity and cruelty. Such cities are portrayed under the figure of Babylon in Revelation 17 and 18.

This confidence in the school as a socializing medium appears also in the concern that the Christian school will not give children sufficient exposure to the non-Christian world. Unless they go to school with children from non-Christian homes they will not relate to and be able to evangelize non-Christians.

This question touches upon an enrolment policy which will be considered elsewhere. For the moment the important point is the belief that people learn to relate to other people simply by being with them. This conviction flows from Dewey's belief that if a man is put in a situation where he is exposed to problems and difficulties, he will overcome them. It is supposed that man will be keen to solve his problems. Place him in a situation that has a problem and he will solve it. Hence a child placed with other children will learn to relate to them. In this 'Christian' adaptation of a non-Christian idea, this relating goes to the point of evangelizing them.

What has been completely ignored in the whole argument are the values and attitudes the child brings to the situation. If a child comes from a home that has taught love and kindness to all men, then he will relate to others of a different group. If he comes from a home of prejudice and selfishness then mere proximity to a hated group will not change the situation. That is not to say there is no advantage to be drawn from contact with others. We are to put into effect what we are taught. If our contact with others gives us opportunity to do that, then it is good for us.

The school, it must also be said, should not be the only place where a child experiences such exposure. If his only knowledge of people of beliefs, classes and races different from his own is through his school, then it says something not complimentary about his home and his church. Instead of saying that children have to be sent to state schools so they can learn to evangelize, we adults should be showing them how evangelism is engaged in through our example. To shift the responsibility for evangelism on to the children is a measure of our failure. As an extension of the Christian home the school will require that people of all backgrounds are treated with love.

'HANDS-ON' EDUCATION

One consequence of the belief that children learn by doing has been an emphasis on activity. This can take various forms. When it is combined with romanticism it can lead to a bias against what is theoretical and abstract. Thus you will come across people who argue that the pupil may as well be taught basket-weaving as mathematics. Some will say that it is wrong to show esteem to the child who does well in mathematics over and above that shown to the child who does well in some activity like basket-weaving.

We are looking here at different abilities. What we find in Scripture on this subject deals principally with the difference of abilities used to edify the church (1 Corinthians 12–14). Yet there are certain important principles on which this teaching is based. Since all gifts are from God, to have a particular gift does not make one person better than another. A person may have a particular gift and not be very mature as a believer. Nevertheless certain gifts have a functional utility. Thus Paul encourages prophesying because of its usefulness to the church.

Rationalism sees the ability to think and reason abstractly as a higher gift. It is higher because the salvation of mankind is believed to come through such abilities. Romanticism naturally reacts against this, but is inclined to do the same thing another way by giving the same esteem to the artistically gifted. As Christians we do not see people as superior or inferior in terms of the ability they possess. God will assess how well they have used that ability. Yet we can still make judgments as to the practical usefulness of various abilities. We may choose to give more time in the curriculum to mathemathics than to basket-weaving. That is because we see more ways in which math-ematics is useful to a wider range of people. It does not mean that a child with mathematical ability is intrinsically superior to one without it.

This emphasis on activity also shows itself in the belief that a child will learn more by manipulating things and seeing their relationships rather than by word-of-mouth instruction. Once again a pragmatic justification can be given for this position. It is argued that children remember better what they have learned for themselves in actual experience. This point was touched upon in the previous chapter. It is an area where generalizations are dangerous. We need to take specific cases.

Can a child learn much about pottery and never actually work with clay? It would be hard to imagine somebody suggesting that this was possible. Yet even in the teaching of pottery there are variations in the relation of instruction and practice. Should one give a child clay and tell him to make a pot or should one demonstrate techniques and then have the child practise them? A true romantic or a true convert to the Dewey method might opt for the first possibility. That is because their fundamental concern is not that the child should learn to make pots. The romanticist is primarily concerned that the child should be helped to express his native originality without the interference of another's style or technique. The disciple of Dewey wants the child to be confronted with a problem he must overcome. For them the pot is really unimportant.

For the Christian however, although the finished product is important, his first concern is that the child should learn to produce something which will be useful to another or give pleasure to another. The child's self-expression is not more important than his service to others. It makes sense, therefore, to learn from a person who already knows how to make a pot.

There is a further issue here which relates to the difference in ability amongst children. A teacher knows how children with no previous experience would fare if given clay and told to make a pot. He may suspect that some would do much better than others. For some the experience would be intensely discouraging. They would have no idea how to proceed and the result would be total discouragement that would turn the child away from the activity. We must have a real compassion for the child who thinks he is poor at a certain activity.

Dewey's method assumes a high level of ability. We may suppose that the teacher is present and will help those who are having difficulty. Yet the explanation of the same thing individually to a dozen children is time-consuming. Some children will be missed out through lack of time or simply overlooked. The discouraged child will fear to ask for the help he needs lest he draw further attention to his own inability.

What is said for pottery applies to many subjects. To assume initial ability and competence in the child is very discouraging for the child who does not have that initial ability. It is far better to explain initially the basic techniques and allow a child to practise them until he has gained a measure of ability. Obviously the time comes when the child should attempt new things for himself. But the time to do this is *after* he has acquired some degree of confidence and skill.

Let us take a very different example. A word like 'suspect' may be stressed on either the first or the second syllable, depending on whether it is used as a noun or a verb. Assuming we want the child to know this, how should he learn it? One way would be to give the child a large number of such words and have him say them in various contexts. He could then be asked to determine where the stress was falling. Alternatively the teacher could give the general rule and have the pupil practise with such words in different usages to learn how the rule worked.

Is one way superior to the other? Unless clear directive hints and clues are given, a primary child is unlikely to realize the purpose of the first exercise. To him it is boring and purposeless. Hence he will take a long time to come to the right conclusion. One can give him very direct hints but to do so is only a variant on the second approach.

There are several reasons why it makes sense to follow an approach which explains a fact or relationship rather than to expect children to work such things out for themselves. One reason is related to time. Effectively many schools have a very narrow curriculum. It is restricted by concentration on the world of the child's experience. It is restricted also in that the aim is not to develop a wide range of abilities. It has become restricted to the development of a certain sort of character; either the free individual of romanticism or the problem solver of Dewey.

Christians, however, approach character development in a different fashion. Instruction in the truth of God's Word is their method. The school wants to develop abilities and competencies, indeed a wide range of competencies, and time is important. If the child learns more quickly by direct instruction, that is an important consideration. Why waste the child's precious time in school by sending him on a search when he does not really know what he is looking for? Certainly he needs the experience of seeing and working with a relationship in action. He can have that once he knows what it is all about.

A further consideration is money. To learn by discovery requires much equipment. It tends to lead to a dependence upon textbooks with multitudinous exercises and blanks to be filled in. It is a method that developed in an age of affluence. That age has passed. Finances are generally very tight in a Christian school. One may scorn 'chalk and talk' teachers but they are economical. For the teacher's salary is the same whether he talks or not, and chalk is cheaper than textbooks. The state school is not worried about such considerations. The Christian school has to bear them in mind, lest Christian schooling be denied to the poor. It cannot simply raise its fees and make itself a school for the wealthy only. That is contrary to God's concern for the poor.

It is not claimed that the discovery method is always wrong.

Obviously sometimes it is appropriate. It is a question of which is the basic instructional method – discovery or teacher instruction. That is, do we integrate investigatory tasks into a framework provided by what the child has been taught by mature Christian teachers or do we use instruction as secondary to the child's own discovery-learning? The distinction is crucial because it reflects fundamental differences between Christian and non-Christian thought.

๑ 5 ๑

Teaching

Teaching can be viewed as something so simple that one cannot understand why so many children do not learn. Or it can be seen as something so complex and demanding that it is a wonder anybody succeeds in it at all. It could be seen as something one can do just by courses with a certain title. Or it can be seen as a gift you either have or you do not have.

Each school of educational theory has its own definition of what teaching is. Yet there are certain things on which they all seem to agree. Rationalism has largely triumphed in respect of the way in which men and women are trained to be teachers. They are taught theoretical educational psychology and educational philosophy. The premise is that the empirical study of how children function and learn will enable teachers to teach them the 'natural' way. Similarly educational philosophy strives to create the perfect rational analysis of education.

There is a story, which may be apocryphal but could well be true, about a Scottish university. There was a proposal to add a department of Education to the Arts Faculty. This created strong opposition from some quarters within the faculty. They insisted that a university was for theoretical study and should not become a mere college for teaching the techniques of education. They were solemnly assured, however, that education as taught at the university level was a theoretical discipline quite divorced from what goes on in the classroom. That could describe many tertiary courses in education. Teachers use very little, if anything, of what they are taught in educational psychology or philosophy.

The reason for the practical uselessness of these subjects is

[61]

obvious. Rationalism is wrong. You cannot start with rats in mazes or salivating dogs and come to a complete understanding of a child. You cannot lock his stages of learning into a necessary sequence on the model of the organism progressing from one stage of evolution to another, because the child is made in the image of God. There is a measure of order and regularity in the child's behaviour and learning, for he is a creature. Yet the child still retains the mystery of a person.

Thus it is not that it is wrong to seek by observation to understand children. It is that the reductionist and evolutionary assumptions built into much educational psychology ruin it. The sort of observations that are useful are those made by good teachers who have had years of experience. They are not the abstract and theoretical sort the rationalist wants.

Thus teachers are trained by receiving courses which are likely to be misguided and unlikely to be useful. Education departments seem reluctant when it comes to curriculum matters to admit that the various approaches current are mere reflections of competing philosophical schools. That reluctance can be traced back to another factor. There is strong scepticism in the general community about philosophy. The various schools have been at work for hundreds of years and have not been able to solve the problems of man. To admit that a certain curriculum approach was an application of romanticism would not be likely to commend it. Hence teachers are either told that a certain approach is the quintessence of education wisdom and all who do not use it are ignoramuses, or they are confronted with the competing array and told to take a little bit of each. Both approaches leave the teacher without adequate basis for judgment.

Yet for all this, the educational establishment strives hard to create a mystique about education. It knows that there is strong public disillusionment with education. Education competes for the increasingly tight financial resources of governments. If teaching is something anybody can do without special and formal training, then the status of those who have been trained formally is diminished and the status of those who train them is also diminished. Against this threat 'Education' has to be promoted as an esoteric discipline which requires special training.

This is not an argument against the training of teachers. It is simply to point out that much which goes by that name is useless.

[62]

If the teacher thinks such a course has made him an 'expert' he is doubly confused.

In Christian schools the problem is more often a recognition that teacher training has proved very deficient. The problem is then to know what one should put in its place. There are a number of simple things which can be done.

EXPLAIN

A fundamental role of the teacher is to explain. This might seem self-evident but it is important to realize that the schools of educational method so far considered de-emphasize, or even oppose, explaining. The rationalist does so because he believes the correct arrangement of material will make explanation unnecessary. Furthermore, the rationalist is generally enamoured of his theoretical jargon. He does not want to break his jargon down, explain and simplify it. He simply wants the pupil to learn his system. The romanticist does not want the teacher to explain lest he impose adult categories on the child. The follower of Dewey wants the child to discover it for himself so the teacher is not encouraged to explain.

Further, teachers have generally been taught at a crucial point of their preparation by people who use fairly technical and abstract language. The tertiary lecturer is generally using a very different style from that which a teacher needs to use. Hence the teachers have lacked models for an explanatory role.

When a teacher has himself been taught at school by a method which did not involve explanation, then there are additional consequences. Once more the teacher is lacking a model. Teaching methods which do not involve explaining can lead to a good student having an intuitive feel of the material without that material being known and fully understood. When that student later becomes a teacher he may have trouble giving an explanation of material he himself does not fully understand. He will expect his pupils to learn as he did, by intuition without the material being explained.

Explaining involves breaking the material down into small steps. Many children who are said not to be able to grasp a certain concept, can do so if they are taught in small stages and if various parts of the problem are isolated and taught sequentially. Learning by discovery tends to present a complex situation to a child, trusting in the child's ability to recognize the significant elements of that complex. Children often find that very hard to do. Explaining is the art of selecting the parts of the problem and making sure each is understood before proceeding to the next. As the child's ability grows, the elements being selected naturally become larger.

One can break the material down, simply because there is order in the creation. Once again it needs to be stressed that we do not see order as the rationalist does. It is not an exhaustive theoretical order. Nevertheless there is regularity. It needs to be stressed also that many teachers have come through a romanticist training with very strong bias against analysis. Therefore this approach may be strange to many teachers.

Explaining also involves illustration. The classic example of this is Scripture. In this matter the church can be of aid to the teachers. Good preaching and teaching in the church generally involves illustration. If the teacher sees a model in the church it may help to compensate for the lack of models in his own education.

Rationalism, being abstract and theoretical, is generally averse to illustration. Further, the rationalist, believing truth to be self-evident, does not see the need for illustration. Teachers who have come out of such an environment must give time to thinking of illustrations, comparisons, stories, demonstrations and such like, to get the point across. Later it will come more naturally.

Explaining involves repetition. Repetition is important for fixing something in the mind and making it available for instant recall. It is also necessary for the child who does not learn quickly. Once again we must have compassion for the pupil who has problems. That child will often learn provided something is repeated. Of course attention has to be given to making the repetition interesting and purposeful. If the teacher sees no point in repetition he will convey that to the class and they will see it as boring. If the teacher sees purpose in it and works at it, then the reaction of the child will be different.

The extension of repetition is memorization. You only memorize what you think is so important that you want it perfectly at your fingertips. The romanticist will, of course, claim that nothing is worth memorizing because nothing the adult tells the child has lasting worth. In the strong bias against memorization in today's education we see something of the strength of romanticism.

There is an important side-effect of memorization. It develops the ability to memorize. Certain professions, for example engineering, where it is useful to retain formulae in the memory rather than consult a book on the job, are now finding a problem. Engineers, who have come through an education opposed to memorization, have great trouble in memorizing what is desirable. Another consequence is inability to memorize Scripture.

The loss of ability to memorize affects the tests that schools can give children. If the child lacks the ability to absorb and remember information, then testing is very difficult. Often schools try to compensate for this by reducing the material to be tested. For example, instead of a year's material the test may be applied to a month's material. This, however, affects curriculum. Courses which require time to build concepts or information tend to disappear and to be replaced by more packaged, less conceptual courses. That is an educational loss. The child finds it then much more difficult to cope with major examinations at high school or tertiary level.

MOTIVATE

Children need to be motivated to work at learning. For learning necessitates work. It can be difficult, discouraging work. The prime motivation is that God requires it of us. The teacher needs to keep this fact before the child. State schools are forced to seek for alternative motivations. They tend to use self-centred reasons. They will argue that a child should do well at school in order to make money later. Or they will try to use rewards to encourage learning. In a subsidiary way these things may enter into a Christian motivation. We may say a child needs to learn in order to make money, but the money is to support others as well, for example the family and the needy. And we are to use our money that way because God tells us to do so. Ultimately it comes back to our responsibility to God out of gratitude for what he has done for us.

The use of rewards as a motivation is a debated subject. Some schools give material rewards. Others give psychological rewards, for example, commendation. Others again give prestige for academic accomplishment. Against this there are those who are against giving any reward lest children work for the wrong reason.

The Book of Ecclesiastes is relevant for this issue. Ecclesiastes also speaks to an issue which is quite common amongst students. Some students cannot complete their work because they must have it perfect. Ecclesiastes points out the futility of the human search for final perfection and final accomplishment. Yet it also has another message. A man is to see good in his labour (2:24). Ecclesiastes is dealing with the practical equivalent of the debate between rationalism and romanticism that was considered earlier. The perfectionist wants to have the perfection and finality of God. He is not willing to accept creaturely limitations. A reaction to the failure of this attempt is to say that there is no point whatsoever in work. But to work is undoubtedly beneficial to both man and child. We all gain from a sense of accomplishment and achievement. We need to see good in our labour. So the child needs to be commended for the work he has done. He needs that sense of satisfaction. Since he is a child and has trouble gauging the standard of his own work, he needs the teacher to commend work that has been done well.

Behaviourism has distorted the whole issue of rewards. The behaviourist sees man as an animal. An animal responds to immediate material rewards. Hence man is seen as responding in a similar way. Given man's material needs, and in particular his sinful cravings, he will often work for material rewards. However, the behaviourist ignores all the other aspects of man's character. He does not see that man, made in the image of the Creator, needs to work at something and to accomplish something. The behaviourist will stress the material reward and ignore the satisfaction of work accomplished. Generally speaking the most needed reward is the praise and encouragement of a respected and loved teacher or parent. Schools which substitute material rewards for this show a lack of understanding of children.

Related to this issue is the question whether children's work should be marked and whether that mark should be divulged to the children. A romanticist will reject marking out of hand. Some Christians are opposed to the divulging of marks on the ground that it tends to breed sinful pride and competition. That is certainly a valid concern. They also make the point that children who do not perform well academically may be discouraged, even though they have done well in other, perhaps more important, areas. To give marks for work can tend to the elevation of particular skills to the detriment of others.

[66]

These are valid points. Yet we need to be careful of falling into the reverse trap. A school which selects certain pupils to represent it in a sporting competition has done the same thing as marking, for it has recognized that these particular children have outstanding ability in that area.

Paul, in a context where he is talking about the different abilities God has given to the church, points out the need to have a proper and sound assessment of our own abilities. We are not to over-rate them (Romans 12:3). This is an area in which we all struggle and children struggle also. We need to help them to realize that there are tasks at which they excel, and tasks which they find troublesome. A teacher must learn to appreciate the child who has abilities that he or she lacks. To the extent that marking gives a child help in assessing how he is doing, it can be defended. We have to be alert to the problems of pride, competition, and discouragement which may result. Where a child has done well, he needs the extra reinforcement of personal commendation. Where he has done poorly he needs help either to accept lack of ability in that area or to work harder.

Marking can also help the child, and especially the parent, to assess the child's progress towards the goal of school education. The school is not an independent entity. It must communicate with the parents and often does so by issuing periodical reports on behaviour, ability, and success or otherwise.

The discussion of the problems that come with marking reinforces a point made earlier. The rewards of behaviourist systems cannot take such problems into account. The personal commendation can be slanted to deal with these problems, whereas tangible rewards or elevation to some higher stage of work cannot perform the same service.

A MODEL

All the time a teacher is teaching he is under examination. His character is analysed. His fairness is examined. His inconsistencies are probed. That is why teaching is such a test of character. The teacher gives orders and sets tasks. Those under orders will react to any hint of hypocrisy.

As far as curriculum is concerned, there is a very important sense in which the teacher is a model. There is strong pressure on

Christians to live as though Christianity is practically irrelevant. As far as schooling is concerned this shows itself in a clear separation between secular academic content and Scripture. The teacher has to be the model of one who has striven and laboured to interpret all his work and effort from a biblical point of view. If he has not completely succeeded, that is not a problem. We are not perfect. If it is not obvious that he is working to the limit of his powers, there is a great problem. For he is teaching the children by example that Christianity and academic disciplines can be separated.

Many Christian educators on the tertiary level may be opposed to Christian schooling and committed to the state school system. Others are consciously or unconsciously worried by charges that the Christian school system is educationally inferior. They see the state school system as the standard. Thus they are basically committed to the state system. That means being tied to a curriculum and educational methodology that is not Christian.

Yet people at large know that there is to be something different about the Christian in education. If it cannot be curriculum or methodology, then what is it? They seek the answer in the realm of personal relationships. They say that a Christian teacher of children should be outstandingly loving and kind. That is certainly true, but it is only part of the story. Such love and kindness should characterize every believer. It is not the distinguishing mark of teaching. It is not the sole thing that separates the Christian and the non-Christian teacher. The content of instruction must also be different. The methodology must be consistent with biblical teaching. The example the teacher should set has to be an example which applies to every aspect of life, public and private.

DISCIPLINE

The area of discipline represents a major problem for teachers. We must remember that we are influenced by the approaches of non-Christian educational systems. We need to think through our Christian basis for what we do.

First we must keep clear the distinction between the results of sin and sin itself. For example, if a child is blind, then his being blind has some connection with sin. He lives in a fallen world. Yet he may not be personally responsible for his blindness. We could not hold him responsible if there was something he did not learn because he was blind.

Similarly there are many other physical causes of failure to learn. We cannot hold a child responsible or punish a child for them. Nevertheless not all failures to learn are due to some physical problem over which the child has no control. They may be due to something for which the child is accountable, as, for example, failing to study when told to do so.

Horror stories are sometimes told about schools in former days, as, for example, the caning of children who failed a test. The problem here is that the distinction has not been made between failure due to circumstances beyond the child's control and failure due to disobedience.

In practice, when it comes to school performance, it may be very difficult to assess the causes. Is the child to blame or not? A child with physical problems is often indulged and so will have behaviour problems as well. Conversely a child may discover that he escapes work by pretending to have a problem. Often the problems are so intertwined that it takes considerable skill to distinguish them.

In practice, the areas where a teacher needs to exercise various forms of discipline are not so much failure in academic work as in the practices or attitudes which cause that failure. Or it may be practices which occur at school time but are unrelated to schooling. One thinks here of problems that arise in the playgrounds. Basically, evil practices can be described as disobedience either directly to the commandments of God or indirectly to those in legitimate authority under God.

Non-Christian educational systems are facing the consequence of destroying the moral basis of parental authority. They are faced with very serious moral and behaviour problems. Yet they do not believe there is any absolute right or wrong. They are forced to define sin as anti-social or inappropriate behaviour. They attempt various behaviour modification techniques and yet the crucial factor is lacking, namely, the knowledge and conviction as to the differences between right and wrong.

Discipline must start with the teacher's conviction that certain behaviour is wrong. If the teacher is not sure of that he will not discipline effectively. He will discipline to his own convenience

[69]

and the children will sense his inconsistencies. Further, he cannot give an adequate explanation to the children of his standards of discipline.

If we start with Scripture then we see that Scripture not only tells us what is right and wrong. It also shows variation in punishments. That is not to say we can learn from Scripture what should be the punishment for a particular misdemeanour on the part of a child. Yet we should not treat every sin as of equal gravity.

This point is made to temper and put in perspective important biblical instruction. The Book of Proverbs sees corporal punishment as appropriate for the child (13:24; 22:15; 23:13, 14). To respond to each misdemeanour with the same physical punishment is to ignore the gradation in the seriousness of sin found in Scripture. On the other hand, to see physical punishment as the very last resort, never to be used except in some rare and extreme circumstance, is not taking Proverbs seriously. Each school needs to come to some sort of consistency in its disciplinary practices. It is worth considering policies in which clear disobedience or wrong to others receives corporal punishment. The problem caused by a policy in which corporal punishment is tried only after everything else has been tried and has failed, is that serious sins are not treated with the remedy Scripture recommends.

The strong opposition to corporal punishment today comes from several factors. One is the belief in the fundamental goodness of the child. Obviously if the child is good, punishment is quite inappropriate. Another factor has already been mentioned: the misuse of punishment as a universal reaction to failure.

The whole subject of discipline has been confused by behaviourism. Behaviourism has no real moral basis. It treats man as an animal whose behaviour is to be modified by suitable punishments. The punishment is thus not adapted to the seriousness of the sin. One practical result of behaviourist schemes of behaviour modification is often a descent into the trivial and the ridiculous. A whole series of trivial punishments is set up that endlessly postpone the moment of effective discipline. Because man is seen as basically an animal there is no incentive to give a reason for him to change. He is to be changed purely by graduated punishments.

Far better is the biblical way: reasoned rebuke with the reason coming from God's Word, supported where needed by corporal punishment.

[70]

THE TEACHER'S PERSONAL STRUGGLE

Many of a teacher's problems are not with curriculum or methodology. They are with himself. That is not to say that all failure in teaching is due to a teacher having personal problems. Curriculum and methodology play a part. Teachers are also often confronted with the consequences of the system which was described earlier. They find themselves undergoing an academic course of teacher instruction without knowing whether they have the aptitude to be a teacher. Sometimes teachers have problems simply because they are following the wrong profession. To face that fact is not failure.

Furthermore, personal problems may mar the teaching of a person who is definitely gifted. One of the problems of the academic approach to teacher training is that it conveys an idea that the teacher who has completed the course is an 'expert'. He has passed the examinations; he must be expert! This attitude is particularly inculcated because of the need to bolster the position of the teacher in a system which is usurping the rights of parents. The teacher has to think of himself in that way to justify his authority. Once a teacher sees himself after this fashion, it is very hard to admit that he still needs to learn.

At this point, and with all the other personal problems a teacher faces, his Christian maturity is put to the test. As Proverbs once again points out, the way to wisdom is to desire and long for it (4:7; 2:3ff.). The person who thinks that he possesses wisdom to the full does not seek for extra wisdom. But he who is truly taught of the Lord recognizes his need for understanding and growth. This work is largely about curriculum. Hence the aspect of the fitness of teachers may easily be minimized. That arises from the concentration of this work; not from what really applies in the school situation. No curriculum will avail if the teacher is not personally appropriate. Further, we should not merely look for some bare and minimal Christian profession in teachers. We should also look for understanding and a clear desire to grow in the things of the Lord. Unless that is there, the teacher will not survive the personal struggles of the classroom. He may do an acceptable job on casual impressions, but the children will lack the personal stimulus of one grappling with problems and overcoming them in the Lord's strength.

Further, he may reject a genuinely Christian curriculum as requiring too much work and as being too different from what is fashionable in contemporary education. The person who is growing does not avoid work and is not desirous of comfortable conformity to the world.

Amongst serious personal difficulties in teachers we need to face the following:

a) *Lack of Personal Organization and Discipline*

Teaching requires organization. The material of lessons must be prepared. The teacher must be punctual. Now obviously there are degrees. One should not go to extremes and have phobias about a single pencil out of place. People with such phobias do not succeed as teachers because their attempt to organize the material world around them is a substitute for being unable to deal with people. Some people come to teaching with a stronger bent for organization than others. Some people tend to be tidier than others. Yet the real question is not what the teacher's study looks like at home. It is whether he is well organized in respect of work in school.

The students will react to the inconsistencies they see in a teacher. If they are expected to be punctual, they are scornful if a teacher is unpunctual. If their work is expected to be completed at a certain time, they are irritable when it is not returned corrected at a certain time.

At the outset a teacher finds this very hard. He has no stock of prepared work. That is quite understandable. All that can reasonably be expected is that progress is being made. The second year should show a marked improvement on the first.

Sometimes circumstances of a personal nature can intrude into a teacher's preparation and marking. That cannot be avoided. Difficulties arise even in a teacher's life. Depending on the age of the children, some brief explanation of them may help the situation. One late arrival of the teacher may well be explained, but if we are perpetually late for our appointments, then our excuses wear thin. If we occasionally run late we feel that the person we have troubled deserves an apology and explanation. Let us remember that children are people deserving similar courtesy.

The sort of curriculum that is developed in this book puts a particular strain on the teacher's organizational gifts. Curricula in which children supposedly teach themselves are less demanding.

Some organization is required initially to have materials for children to work on. Sometimes this comes pre-packaged for the teacher. Where the teacher is actually teaching it is much more difficult. The teacher has to prepare to introduce and explain. He has to do so in such a way that the class as a whole can understand. And he needs materials prepared on which students can practise concepts and skills.

Lack of organization is also a problem in a teacher's use of his holiday time. One of the community perceptions of teachers is that they have many more holidays than anybody else. If they genuinely do, then they will often meet with trouble in teaching. A typical situation is that a teacher begins his first year with very little material prepared. That is not his fault. It is largely the fault of his training. Hence, if he is conscientious, he works night and day just to keep up with the class. By the time the holidays come, he rightly feels he has earned a good rest. However, if he uses all such rest-periods as holidays he will find himself in a somewhat unprepared state at the beginning of the next year. Thus the next year will also be taxing. So a cycle develops of overwork at some stages of the year and exhaustion at others. It also intensifies any existing tendencies to do things in a rush at the last moment.

To be an effective teacher, and to have time available for family and other responsibilities, the teacher needs long-term organization. School holidays cater for preparation for the future as well as for recreation.

b) *Stagnation*

The problems of teachers are very real at the start of their career. Yet after some years a reasonably competent teacher builds a store of materials and experience. What then? There is a danger of stagnation. As one looks at the Christian school movement as a whole, in its many decades of existence, there is relatively little available in the way of good, genuinely Christian curriculum material. And yet one knows that there are experienced teachers everywhere at work who have the ability to write curricula.

There are many causes for the lack. Not all blame should be placed on teachers. Often they are caught in a system which pictures the tertiary person as the expert in curriculum matters. Hence their problem is one of confidence. Or they may receive no encouragement from others around them since the other experienced teachers or parents who should encourage are in the same problem or consumed by school administrative burdens.

Nevertheless some of the lack must be due to stagnation. The teacher has found non-Christian materials that are not too offensive in his eyes. Or he is using pre-packaged material that is superficially Christian. As long as he can get by with such material, what incentive does he have to go deeper or to attempt to develop his own materials? A secondary consequence is that the lack of teachers interested in such materials is a disincentive to publishers to market them.

c) *Lack of Authority*

One teacher walks into a classroom. Without his saying a word, hush descends and the children eagerly turn their minds to learning. Another teacher enters the same classroom. By dint of great effort he obtains some measure of control. For all his control the class throughout the lesson seems more likely to burst into open revolt than to learn.

What is it? What is that mysterious something that some teachers obviously seem to have and others lack? We can call it a charisma or a gift and yet it can be developed. Even a very good teacher may not have been so obviously good at the beginning.

There is no one secret. Doubtless it is partly connected to personality. Yet we can say some things about it. Determination is a major part. The good teacher is determined that the child must and shall learn. The rebellious and mischievous child senses that if he resists then he will be opposing all the power, forces, and energy the teacher can command.

It is not merely determination. Tyrants have that, yet they are poor teachers. It is also selflessness. The determination is for the good of the child, not just for the teacher's good. A good teacher tends to be an open and generous person.

Can such qualities be nurtured and developed? Determination is much related to conviction. A true conviction is founded on a confidence in Scripture. Teachers with a clear sense of what is right and wrong have a much easier task with discipline. They must possess the determination to succeed as a teacher. If one sees that as his responsibility to God, then it gives him extra incentive. It helps overcome one of the crucial problems of teachers: fear of public exposure. Teaching involves a projection of oneself. As much as an actor on the stage, a teacher projects himself into the public arena. Many teachers find such a projection hard to accomplish. Their style is withdrawn and tentative.

If a man walks down the street shouting and talking very loudly, we note him as having a problem. He is trying to draw attention to himself. If there is a fire and he walks down the street calling out the warning in a subdued and tentative voice, we would also say he has a problem. An extrovert is a bad teacher if his extroversion is selfishly motivated. His concern is himself and not the children. An introvert may also be a bad teacher if the introversion has a selfish motivation. He is then refusing to project his personality for fear of exposure to ridicule and embarrassment.

Many of the other problems we have considered – tardiness, disorganization, etc. – stem from a basic selfishness in the teacher. Other priorities, especially those which are personal, are more important in his eyes.

Here we meet with spiritual problems. The answer lies in placing responsibility to God and concern for the children above oneself. That can only come when the fact of God's unselfishness in giving his Son for us has taken control of us.

THE TEXTBOOK TEACHER

Few cooks today prepare everything starting from the most basic ingredients. There may be a few who start with wheat and grind their own flour, make their own bread, tomato sauce, and so on. Most make use to a greater or lesser extent of pre-prepared materials. At the other extreme to the cook who starts with his own wheat is the one who simply heats frozen dinners bought in the supermarket.

Similarly teachers vary in the extent to which they rely upon prepared and textbook material. Some do little more teaching than telling the child the starting page in the textbook. Others may do more teaching but have allowed the textbook to shape the curriculum, rather than using textbooks as they fit into the curriculum.

One can sympathize with the teacher's reliance on the textbook, especially when he is inexperienced. Many teachers in Christian schools teach multiple-grade classes. That increases the preparation time and organizational demands. In order to survive, a teacher may feel it necessary to rely upon textbooks, at least for part of the course.

The problems of textbook reliance are connected to the lack of good Christian texts but they go further. The textbook easily becomes a substitute for teaching given by the teacher himself. Then the classroom lacks the personality and interest that is provided by a living teacher in interaction with the class. A textbook may reinforce a teacher but a textbook cannot replace a teacher. There is also the problem mentioned earlier of a lack of incentive for people to produce Christian texts. If the Christian school teachers have become dependent upon the existing non-Christian or superficially Christian texts, what incentive is there to produce Christian texts of good quality?

Given the demands upon teachers it is unreasonable to expect them to teach without textbooks. However, one would hope to see a lessening of the dependence as the teacher becomes more experienced. We require such independent teachers for the sort of curriculum which is recommended in this book. It is a curriculum for which texts do not presently exist. Teachers dependent upon textbooks will naturally be dismayed at that prospect. If we are to develop really Christian curricula then we must become the masters of the textbooks, using them where possible and yet controlling the course. Otherwise there will never be thoroughly Christian curricula.

THE IMPERATIVE OF GROWTH

We cannot pretend that the task of being a Christian teacher is an easy one. Nobody starts as a mature, wise, and experienced teacher. Even experienced teachers, if they are not stagnant, are constantly re-evaluating what they are doing, and adjusting it. To expect instant perfection is unreasonable and discouraging. What we should be expecting is growth. The teacher is like the child. The child needs to see evidence that he is learning, that he is making progress. So the teacher for his own encouragement needs to know that he has matured. A teacher with that encouragement projects to the class the example and the enthusiasm of one who is also a learner.

‿ 6 ‿

Relationships within the School Community

This chapter is in part an admission of the fact that curriculum is but one factor in the running of a successful school. Even the best curriculum will be useless in a school which does not work together as a community.

It is also a recognition of the fact that any Christian school curriculum, and the suggestions in this book in particular, puts a great load on a teacher. The school must be organized to share that load and not to place unnecessary demands on teachers.

The curriculum guidelines recommended in this work have not been developed merely out of theoretical considerations. They have been developed with a view to meeting some of the practical problems that arise in the functioning of a school. Those problems will lead to tensions in the life of the school community. They may not be the largest tensions but they will still be problems.

THE DYNAMICS OF THE COMMUNITY

Ideally the school community should be just that: a community! However, when the community tends to break down, it will follow the pattern that is common in our society, that is into a polarization of parents and teachers. Where the school is administered by a board, that board will also tend to fall on one side or the other of that polarization. Hence it is advisable to examine that polarization. We can look at it either from the perspective of parents viewing teachers or teachers viewing parents.

A lot of the polarization has to do with the attitude that the teacher is the expert and the parents are really ignoramuses. There can also be a parental reaction to this. If a parent has felt that teachers as a whole look down upon him, he may react with an assertion of superiority in those areas in which he feels superior to the teacher. Since many teachers are relatively young, and often inexperienced in the administration of a school, the parent may assert that superiority.

Alternatively the parents may simply accept the common idea and regard the teachers as the experts in education. In many ways that is a convenient idea. It absolves the parent from any responsibility to think about educational matters. A cleavage may stem from the idea that parents provide the money and teachers are left to provide the education as they please. This is just as bad as the polarization mentioned earlier. The teachers are then no longer working with the parents. Rather, the parents have given up all their responsibilities. The point of conflict in such cases is often associated with finance. The parents do not understand enough of what the teachers are trying to do to see why money is needed for particular materials. Also the teachers may lose touch, especially if they do not have children of their own, with the practical realities. They may demand more, simply to make their job easier or to go along with the fashions of the day, without realizing the financial strain they place upon families.

Whether the parents have found an area in which they can assert their control, or the teachers are just unrealistic, the teachers tend to react to the money problem with a conviction that parents are mean and uncaring. This can be particularly the case if, as in some Christian schools, the teacher's wage is already below that of the comparable state school teacher.

If we are not to be caught unwittingly in these various dynamics we must remember a few simple things. Education is a domain in which those who are supposedly experts are not capable of doing all that is required and desired. Its goal is the bringing of children to maturity in Christ. If that requires the gifts of the whole church community, it will not require anything less in the school community.

Further, we are to have an attitude of compassion and sharing towards one another. Whether it is teachers demanding more equipment or materials or staff, without concern for what that does to the finances of families, or parents living in affluence while teachers receive an inadequate wage, we are doing wrong.

When Christian schools break down it is commonly because of problems in this whole area. The teacher cannot take advice from parents or direction from the school board. That direction may have in it an element of reaction to the feeling of inferiority which educators like to instil in parents. Or the control may pass to teachers and the school become more and more conformed to the educational fashions of the non-Christian schools.

Opponents of Christian schools draw attention to such break-downs as an argument against Christian schools. It should be pointed out that the dynamic that destroys such schools is the dynamic which is taken for granted in state schools, namely, the exclusion of the parent from any say in education by the 'expert' teacher. The flight of parents from state schools is partly caused by that exclusion. Christian schools break up. State schools are content to suffer a constant haemorrhage. It has been pointed out that often the conflict point is money. State schools have largely been saved from this conflict by the willingness of politicians to spend tax revenue willingly on schools. That era is passing. State schools are trying to find ways to extract more money directly or indirectly from parents. Those parents may soon demand more right to be heard.

Finally, inasmuch as Christian schools succeed, as is the case with the vast majority of them, they are overcoming the problem which state schools do not even have the courage to touch. They are making education a co-operative thing. To fail at what is quite beyond the ability of the state system is not a proof of inferiority.

WHAT TEACHERS NEED TO LEARN

In particular curriculum items there is much that individual parents can contribute. Often they will need to be stimulated to consider the relevance of their knowledge and skills for school curriculum. They may have put little thought into a Christian evaluation of the skills and knowledge they use in their own employment. It may necessitate a learning together by teacher and parent. Nevertheless they are a resource which should be utilized.

However, the immediate concern is not with particular curriculum areas, but with more general matters. A large number of teachers have not been parents. Many will not have had smaller brothers or sisters. Thus their experience with children may be minimal and they may have little regard for the typical problems of parents.

This lack of experience manifests itself in many ways. One common symptom is problems in the standard of work to be expected of children, for teachers often set too low a goal for the children they teach. Frequently a teacher does not realize what a small child is capable of, if properly taught and encouraged. This does not mean that the teacher should start at the level of the ultimate goal.

Conversely, teachers are often unaware of the problems created by homework, which requires much time but teaches little in the way of skills or information. This problem is somewhat connected with the idea of learning by doing. To fulfil that aim teachers often give large projects or assignments. Of course homework in the form of a major project can be beneficial to a student. The difficulty arises from the poor planning encouraged by the idea that students can teach themselves. Students may be confronted by a project much bigger than anything they have attempted before. There is no progressive development of the skills required. Often the resources required are not conveniently available in the home. A complication can be that the skills required and the marks awarded can bear little relationship to the allotted topic. For example, a history project may be so constructed that more reward is allotted to the accompanying art-work than to the historical information and skills. It may be objected that this is a good thing, in that it gives students opportunity to use artistic gifts. However, we are considering the project for its educational value. It does not often happen that a history project has been so carefully planned that the art-work required will give opportunity to practise skills which have just been learned in art. When that happens the historical aspect tends to be secondary. In other words we deal here with the problem of integrated themes considered earlier. One discipline tends to predominate and it may not be the announced one.

Where one or more of the above problems emerges, there is a common result. The parent has to step in, often at the last moment, to rescue the project. Where the parent does not do so, the child accomplishes little and is liable to be discouraged.

If parents and teachers have mutually agreed on a project then there is no problem. More commonly the teacher devises the project without consultation. There is thus an intrusion by the school into the family time and resources. Maybe the family routine has to be disrupted in order for the parents to help the child.

The teacher may make assumptions about families which reflect the teacher's own background and tend to impose that upon the school community. For example, the teacher may assume that every home should have a set of encyclopaedias. Such assumptions tend to make poorer families feel unwelcome in a Christian school. Given the Bible's concern for the poor, we cannot act in a way which tends to exclude them.

Of course a teacher who plans well will make sure the resources are available and the skills needed are appropriate. However if he has not had wide experience with a diversity of homes and a diversity of children, he will have a problem. Who better to help him than the parents themselves?

Similarly, teachers are not aware of the financial demands some of their ideas make. For poorer families this can be a major problem.

Some schools make various forms of extra-curricular sport or social activity virtually compulsory. There is once again an intrusion into family time. If a teacher is single he may have time on his hands. Hence he does not appreciate that families, especially Christian families, are busy, and that time is valuable. A form of education which demands much homework needs to be evaluated for its interference with domestic arrangements. The idea of the child teaching himself has spawned a lot of busy work of dubious educational value.

Furthermore, parents often see problems before teachers are aware of them. If there is no free communication between parents and teachers, or if teachers cannot receive advice in such matters, then there will be tensions and dissatisfaction.

WHAT PARENTS NEED TO LEARN

The education which goes on in the home tends to have an informal character. The parents do not plan lessons. Yet considerable learning takes place because of the time the child spends with the parents and the special nature of the relationship.

Given this, the parents may not realize what is involved in school teaching. They may have no real notion of the amount of planning and preparation necessary. They may be quite ignorant of the techniques of formal, as opposed to informal, teaching. Having had no problem in disciplining their own children, they may have no sympathy for the teacher faced with a class of thirty children, all total strangers to him. Alternatively, having had problems with their own children, they regard the teacher who can keep thirty children working as a magician whose ways are beyond comprehension.

These various examples of lack of understanding show the need for communication. If the teacher does not explain what he is doing and why he is doing it, then it is no wonder that parents misunderstand. We must be on our guard against a vicious circle. If the teacher sees what he does as a special discipline, understandable only to the specially trained, he will not try to explain it to the ordinary parent. If the parent then shows a lack of understanding and appreciation of his work, the teacher feels hurt. Instead of blaming himself for the lack of understanding, the experience can reinforce his sense of being different from, and above, the parents.

STRUCTURES WHICH HELP

The need is for communication, explanation, and mutual understanding. The school community should seek ways to facilitate this communication. It is worthwhile to have meetings where teachers explain how and what they are seeking to teach, where they explain the rationale of the curriculum or particular parts of it. Sometimes the attendance of parents at such meetings can be disappointing but the school must persevere. Similarly, the materials a school sends home with children should increase parents' understanding of what the school is doing.

Conversely, the more frequently teachers are welcomed into homes to see something of how a home operates, the more realistic their assignments will be. It is also beneficial for teachers to know something of the operation of the school board. To see the work of board members on behalf of a school can help teachers feel less like martyrs.

It may also give teachers a better idea of the financial constraints under which Christian schools operate. Christians have tended to take over structures and curricula developed by non-Christians. These are usually expensive because the non-Christians have assumed that the resources of the state will be freely available to schools. Teachers need a sense of the financial situation of the school. Elementary financial facts can easily be overlooked. For example, a school cannot increase its expenditure once fees and a budget have been set. That places an onus upon the teacher to plan well ahead for the materials he will need. Thus there is a good reason for teachers to be present as observers at board meetings. They can always be excused if confidential matters arise.

In short the more parents and teachers know of each other's struggles and objectives, the better for the harmony of the school.

THE ISSUES WHICH DIVERT

Much of the time of the school community may be consumed with issues which are important and yet often not as important as the less obvious concerns which have just been discussed. It is not unusual for a meeting of parents to spend three hours on pupil dress and five minutes on curriculum. We need to try to move some of the less important items off the community agenda so that more important issues can be considered.

a) *Behaviour*

It may seem strange to call behaviour an unimportant item. In many ways it is not unimportant. What can be time-consuming and divisive is disagreement on the standards and style of behaviour expected. Some want an almost military standard of respect and conformity from the children. Others favour a much more relaxed style. These differences can lead to argument.

First of all, we must be biblical. We may have to labour long to overcome some problems in children. Most parents can testify to the long battle to deal with sibling rivalry and jealousy, selfishness, and other evils. Yet these things can never be accepted. They may be common in children but they are not right.

The greater problems come with things which are not necessarily wrong. For example, how much boisterous behaviour do we tolerate in children? When they are in class and working, then obviously it is inappropriate and distracting. What of the playground? We have biblical principles by which we can exclude behaviour which is dangerous or so loud as to be bothersome to others. Having excluded such behaviour we still have a problem. One person may like children to sound as if they are having fun. Another may desire more dignified and proper behaviour.

How do we resolve such differences? We can only resolve them if we are ruled by Scripture. A consequence of being ruled by Scripture is that these extra-biblical standards do not command much weight with us. We may have our preferences but we do not see them as important enough to cause conflict.

Where people have strong feelings on such non-moral questions they generally reflect the attitudes of a particular class or group in society. As Christians we are to cut across such social divisions. For a Christian school to take a strong stand on these issues will be to divide the Christian community on class lines. That is wrong.

Hence there are some issues in which the community must refuse to take sides and must seek to make people put things in perspective. If it fails to do this it will have endless debates on trivial questions.

b) *The Dress of Pupils*

Fashions in school dress vary from country to country. The English custom, reflected also in Australia and New Zealand, is for each school to have its own uniform. In the U.S.A., schools generally do not have uniforms. There have been schools within each system which, on their understanding of Christian principles, have gone against the prevailing custom. Those who reject uniforms, where they are the norm, do so on the principle of allowing each pupil to express his own particular individuality. Those who adopt uniforms against their national trend generally talk in terms of neatness and modesty.

What was said in the previous section is very relevant here. Moral issues are involved and questions of personal taste. On some we can insist; on others we cannot do so.

Whether or not schools should have a uniform is not the most crucial question. More important is whether there is a concern for a standard and a code that reflects biblical concerns. Amongst those basic concerns are the following:

(i) *The importance of the heart*

The Scripture includes teaching on tidiness and cleanliness, but the overwhelming thrust of Scripture's concern is in another direction. It is to warn of the danger of relying on external appearances (Matthew 23:25–28). It also warns that no amount of external discipline of the body is of any use in creating godliness (Col. 2:23). Any idea that the way the external man is adorned will change the inner man is positively unbiblical. Rather, the external is a reflection of what is internal (Matthew 23:26; Proverbs 7:10).

This does not mean that the external can be totally ignored. If it could be ignored, modesty would not be an issue. Rather, the external and internal have to be brought into agreement (1 Timothy 2:9, 10).

Hence we must from the outset reject any idea that we can solve basic spiritual problems amongst children by setting certain standards of dress. The dress standards have to be set for other reasons.

(ii) *Modesty*

Scripture is explicit that the body, including its sexual aspects, is part of God's good creation (Genesis 2:23–25; Proverbs 5:15–23; Song of Solomon 4:1–6; 7:1–9). We must never give the impression that our concern for modesty comes from the belief that sex is evil.

Scripture also requires a concern for modesty and an avoidance of situations where immodesty is the likely result (Genesis 9:20–27; Exodus 20:26).

The Bible warns against attempts at attracting attention by external adornment (1 Timothy 2:9–10; 1 Peter 3:3–4).

What confronts us in our world today is a mode of dress that attracts attention to the sexual aspects of the body. We would not deny that many of those who dress in this way, especially the younger ones, may do so with a certain naïvety, conforming to the crowd. But Christian parents should be teaching their children the great danger of thinking that real and lasting attractiveness lies in the physical realm.

(iii) *Compassion*

Sometimes schools choose uniforms or a dress code without concern for the impact of the decision upon all the members of the community. For example, some items of prescribed dress may cause physical pain and discomfort to certain children. Or the prescribed style may be expensive. For some parents that is not a problem, but for others it increases considerably the burden of sending children to a Christian school.

If we neglect the poor and the weak in our decisions, we have ignored one of the most fundamental concerns of Scripture.

(iv) *Tidiness*

Untidiness may have a moral and spiritual cause. It may also have a physical cause, or it may simply be the case that what one person sees as tidy, another sees as untidy. Unless we keep these possible causes distinct, we shall create confusion.

There can be a despising of the body, an attempt to make it ugly and grotesque. 'Punk' is an example of this. Or untidiness can result from physical immaturity, as in the case of the small boy who has difficulty in tucking his shirt properly into his pants. No doubt small boys can be taught to tuck their shirts in, but it might require less effort and release time for more profitable teaching if we simply do not over-labour the point. If it is physical, growing-up is the best remedy and growing-up requires time. Or it can be a way of drawing attention to oneself as in the open shirt. (Hyper-neatness may also be a form of exhibitionism. Let us not just recognize the spiritual problems when they offend while we ignore the same problems when we find them less offensive.) An inflexible rule which would force us, if consistently enforced, to hound most of the little boys, is useless. The real problems are in upper primary and high school, where tidiness is within the physical capacity of the child, but untidiness is being chosen to convey a message to the world around.

Again, we must also make sure that our definition of tidiness is not merely dictated by what we like because of the conditioning of our own background. We must be especially careful on this because Scripture gives so little attention to the issue. At most there are a couple of passages which make the general assumption that cleanliness is the normal state for the sanctified person (Matthew 23:26; Eccl. 9:8). Where untidiness is mentioned, it is an untidiness springing directly from laziness (Proverbs 24:30–34).

We could perhaps also appeal to the general teaching that we are to give attention to things honourable in the sight of all men (1 Peter 2:12). That might direct us towards a general conformity to the community standard of neatness. It certainly does not bind upon us what only part of the community would consider as neatness.

(v) *Members of a community*

At all times we have to think of the influence of our actions on others. For example, immodesty is wrong both in itself and because it encourages others to lust. Extravagant and expensive dress creates a problem for other children and thus for their families. There is pressure to emulate that dress. The child who cannot dress like that is embarrassed and ashamed (note the principle in 1 Cor. 11:22).

Therefore, whether a school adopts a uniform or not, its standard of dress should reflect these principles. It should demand a dress which is modest, inexpensive, and relatively easy to keep tidy. It should expect that parents will be concerned about the impact of their children's dress upon other children and thus on other families.

c) *Money-Raising*

Money-raising tends to be not so much a point of argument as a time- and energy-consuming occupation. Often the responsibility for this falls upon people who are already taxed with other responsibilities. Hence schools need to consider whether the money raised in this manner is enough to justify the effort or whether there could be better methods.

Often, money raising is part of the problem of the 'hidden fee'. Hidden fees are what many schools resort to, in order to supply the school's financial needs. Parents are confronted with an initial fee. In making the decision to send children to the school, parents budget in terms of this advertised fee. They are then constantly asked for extra money for this item or that item.

A hidden fee is dishonest and misleading. The school owes it to parents to tell them how much it will cost. It creates resentment amongst parents when they are trying to build a happy and unified community. It acts as a discouragement to voluntary donation. People are reluctant to give to an organization which they feel is somewhat dishonestly extracting money from them.

If fund-raising is largely drawing money from the school community itself, then the school community should reconsider the matter. It might be better simply to raise the initial fee.

Where the money is being obtained from outside the community, there may still be a need for reconsideration. Does it take

[87]

the time of people who are needed to organize other aspects of the school? Sometimes the money earned is small in comparison to the time spent.

There are people who cannot contribute to the school in terms of setting the curriculum or administering building projects. Yet they want to make some contribution and fund-raising seems to them a good idea. However, if they expect the whole school community to take part in the activity then it uses the time of people who may be better able to make a contribution in another way. It is far better that those with the time and desire should organize their own fund raising. If they do not use the school, and thus the time of others in the school community, it is even better. There is nothing to stop people setting up their own ways to raise money and donating the result to the school.

MAINTAINING THE COMMUNITY

Often a school community begins with a great burst of enthusiasm, only to lose this enthusiasm within a few years. As enthusiasm wanes, so there is less interest in having a truly Christian school. A fair standard of academic attainment is accepted as a substitute for the continuing search for genuine Christian education.

There are several things we must be conscious of, and work towards, if we are to maintain the school and see it grow in spiritual depth and effectiveness.

a) *Esteem*

Teachers can be giving up much to teach in a Christian school. There may be longer hours. Often there is less pay. They should be respected for their sacrifice. As they become more able teachers, there should also be the esteem due to those who show ability and dedication.

Often Christian schools have the problem of instability of staffing. There may have been poor initial choices of teachers so some do not succeed in teaching. Some may leave for a host of personal reasons, for example because of dissatisfaction with their situation or because of a new challenge elsewhere. Some of these departures we can do nothing about. Some we might like to prevent but should not do so, as in the case of an experienced teacher who leaves an established school to give leadership in a new school. The problem we want to avoid is that of the teacher who leaves because he does not find a return commensurate to his efforts. If a teacher who has problems interprets attempts to help him as lack of appreciation, and leaves his post, then it is sad for him but not the school. Far greater is the loss when a good teacher becomes restless and vacates his post.

Any person whose work largely involves other people has a problem in seeing the rewards for his labour. This can be the case especially with children who generally lack the maturity to appreciate and express thanks for what is being done for them. Hence it is very important that adult members of the school community make sure that good teachers know that their labours are appreciated. The sense of being loved and respected will keep a teacher working, even when other circumstances are discouraging. God commands that we are to love and esteem one another for the labours in which we are individually or collectively involved.

b) *Burn-Out*

When the running of the school, maybe in a difficult situation, falls on a few people there can be eventual discouragement and exhaustion. Some schools have tried to meet this problem by insisting on a rotation of responsibilities. For example, there may be policies preventing people serving continuously on the school board. While one can appreciate the objective, one has to doubt the wisdom of this particular measure. There is no sense in artificially removing a knowledgeable and able person from a place where he is most useful. If the board is constantly changing but the teaching staff is stable, then there is a further consequence. The dominant model and example in our society is the teacher-controlled school. If on the side of the teacher the partnership has continuity but in the case of the board there is no continuity of membership, then control will effectively move to the teachers, aided by the fact that it is the model to which people are accustomed.

We must find another way to solve the problem. The best way is the delegation of responsibilities. There are many good biblical precedents for this (Exodus 18:13–23; Acts 6:1–6).

c) *Building Up the Community*

The suggestion of delegation may be met by the problem that there is a lack of people able and willing to accept responsibility. If that is the case the ultimate blame may rest on the church. There is a sense in which Christian schooling is a product of Christian growth as well as a source of it. As people grow in the Lord they want their children to grow and they are willing to accept the responsibilities involved. If people will not take those responsibilities, it may be because they are not growing in the Lord.

What can the school community do about this problem? The solution is not a numerical expansion of the community. Often this is rather a cause of the problem. To understand the dynamics of this problem we must make a crucial distinction. Schools vary in who they allow into a decision-making position. Some allow all parents an equal say in the running of the school. They may attempt to restrict enrolment to Christian families or they may not. Where the latter is the case, the enrolment policy itself will very quickly undermine the Christian character of the school. Others, whether or not they limit enrolment to Christian families, place restrictions upon membership in the controlling association. For the moment the concern is not the advisability of unrestricted enrolment policies. Some aspects of that question will be considered in the next chapter. The concern is with the controlling association, whether this is the same as the whole parent community or not.

When a school is small and struggling there can be strong temptations to allow people into the controlling association quite indiscriminately. There are several serious consequences. One can be the eventual loss of the Christian character of the school. If we admit non-Christians with a nominal church connection we may lose all the work and effort that has gone into making a Christian school. Another temptation is to admit Christians who do not understand or share the basis and vision of the school. They may desire Christian teachers for their children but have little concern for a distinctively Christian curriculum. This failure to appreciate the need for a Christian educational approach may be linked in turn with ignorance of, or wilful rejection of, certain aspects of scriptural teaching. A few examples from previous chapters may make this point clearer.

If a person rejects biblical teaching on the original sinfulness of the child's heart, he will not see the great error of romanticism. Put theologically, we would say that the doctrine of the total depravity of man has important educational consequences. The earlier consideration of rationalism pointed out that it involves ideas of human rational ability which do not square with Scripture. There are theological positions which assert a fair degree of human ability. Some claim that man's reason has not been influenced by sin. They confine the fall of man to his will and his emotions. They say this in order to say that man can give rational assent to the gospel. In effect they reject the regenerating work of the Spirit of God as being that which opens the mind to the gospel (Ephesians 2:1–10). Their rejection of regeneration is connected to their unwillingness to give a biblical answer to the very important question, Why are some regenerated by the Spirit of God and not others? In other words they reject the biblical doctrine of election (note in Ephesians the teaching on election in chapter 1, especially verses 4–6, as a foundation for the teaching on regeneration in chapter 2. See also Romans 9–11). The idea of evolution has already been mentioned earlier and will arise often in considering specific topics related to the curriculum. The person who accepts evolution will logically be much less critical of many non-Christian curriculum ideas.

So we could go on. The essential point is that there is a direct connection between biblical doctrine and the school curriculum. We cannot maintain the curriculum in the school and say at the same time that those in control need not believe biblical teaching. Hence the admission of people at random into the controlling body is asking for trouble.

There is a further consequence. Just as enthusiasm breeds enthusiasm, so lack of enthusiasm breeds lack of enthusiasm. The indifference of the many, who regard the school as a convenience and see no need for further development in the school programme, will discourage those with the right vision.

Thus the way to go is not simply to make the pool of potential workers larger. It is to persevere in the task of teaching people the basis of the school and its curriculum. To some extent the school may have to do what the church has failed to do, if the church has not educated people in biblical doctrine. However it is always doctrine set in the context of its educational consequences.

The school must also search out people who are able to carry some of its responsibilities and tasks. This requires administrative attention in breaking down complex tasks. Teachers are not the only ones who need to learn how to break the complex into the simple!

[91]

There are two groups of people who are often passed over but who form a valuable resource for schools. They are (1) the unmarried, and (2) older people whose families have grown up, especially retired people. The unmarried often have time available and older people have valuable experience.

c) *Loss of the Sense of Need*

A problem which comes with success, even with relative success, is loss of the sense of the urgency of the need. The crises are past which threatened the very life of the school in its early days. In that situation it becomes difficult to delegate responsibilities to others. If there appears no urgent need, why take more work on yourself?

Part of the solution here has to be to introduce the community to the wider task of the school. That task is not completed when we have a school operating. It is not even accomplished when the school has its own buildings and property. These things seem like the outstanding needs, yet they are not the end. For we must persevere to produce an educational system which is thoroughly Christian. The established schools have a responsibility to encourage and help smaller and struggling schools.

We need to put this wider vision before the community. Often Christian schools are started by a relatively small group of people with the right vision and ideas. The school is a success and attracts other parents. However, the larger vision is not easily transmitted beyond the boundaries of the original core.

ADMINISTRATION AND CONTROL

All human organizations involving sinful men have problems with power. Even the church, established by Christ, has to resist men's desires to dominate. Where there is organization, no matter how informal its structure, there is an opportunity for men to feel the sense of glory and power. A Christian school is no exception. Many problems which appear in Christian schools have their origin in conflicts for control and dominance. Sometimes the push for control comes from a parent or other persons on the board. Sometimes it comes from a teacher or a principal.

If there is such a push then there will often be also the desire to turn the school into a monument to the glory of the one man. And people in general show a reluctance to resist the driving egotist.

The problem of a desire for control is not restricted to Christian schools. Principals, superintendents and inspectors in state schools can show very advanced cases of the same problem.

To deal with such problems we must go back to the basic function of the school. It exists to help Christian parents meet their God-given responsibilities. Where one man, or a group of men, dominate, then the community structure and function have been lost.

Hence it is important that the school community is organized with clear lines of leadership and responsibility. Lack of organization enables men to take control more easily. For if roles and responsibilities are not clear, then it is harder to stop a man taking many roles and more power to himself. Further, there has to be a clear sense of accountability to the community as a whole.

The problems of those who administer do not merely revolve around power. Sometimes the opposite is also involved: a fear to show decisiveness and to assume responsibility. Administrators, whether as paid employees of the school or as board members, face many of the same spiritual problems as those discussed earlier with teachers. In the same way that a teacher may fear the exposure to failure of a 'centre stage' teaching role, so an administrator may fear the public exposure of leadership. The answer is the same in both cases. It is a knowledge that we do everything as unto Christ Jesus our Lord. If we fail and are laughed at, it is no more than he endured for us.

A similar fear lies at the root of procrastination. We put off what we fear doing until fear can so grip us that even the smallest task seems difficult. If we do not overcome such problems we shall remain very poor administrators.

There is another problem that teachers and board members share alike. It is a failure to consult with others. Just as the teacher may go ahead without seeing the need to plan conjointly with fellow teachers, or to keep parents informed, so board members may ignore the responsibility of consulting with the school community. This then leads to conflict within the community. While people will often agree with policies if the reasons have been explained and the alternatives discussed, they will react negatively when things are imposed without discussion.

It is important that we master the art of school administration because otherwise all the load will fall on the teachers, particularly the senior teachers and principals. There are enough loads in

Christian school teaching without the unnecessary load of administration. A certain amount unavoidably falls upon the principal because he is on the spot and outside parties assume he is the administrative head of the school. This is particularly true with government agencies which in any case are inclined to want volumes of paperwork.

It is a waste of a valuable resource to take the senior and most experienced teacher and to make a clerk of him. Others can do the administrative work. He is needed to give educational leadership, to consult with parents, and to assist the less experienced teachers.

If we make senior teachers into bureaucrats we shall fall into the pattern so common in state schools. There a teacher may find difficulty with teaching and no satisfaction with the classroom situation. There are two ways out of the personal dilemma. One is to do more study and eventually become a teacher in a tertiary institution, often teaching teachers! The other is to move up into jobs which are administrative rather than educational. Thus they tend to aim for positions like that of principal. Obviously this is a disaster for the school. If the educational leader does not enjoy teaching, one can imagine the example he sets for the rest of the teachers and the sort of advice they receive from him.

To avoid this situation we should make it clear that senior positions in the school are not an escape from teaching and contact with children. Of course, if somebody is not adapted to teaching, we should assist him in finding another position. It makes no sense to make it a position which involves being a leader of teachers.

7

Evangelism and the Christian School

THE ALTERNATIVE MODEL

So far we have considered the school as an extension of the home. We have considered various ideas dominant in non-Christian education and tried to develop a distinctive Christian methodology. Later we shall consider some specific ideas for a distinctively Christian curriculum.

These emphases are not the only ones found in Christian schools. One commonly finds other reasons put forward for their creation. Prominent among these is the need to shelter children from the influences of the world. Whether we put that high on the list of our reasons for having a Christian school, we have to admit that it is high on many parents' lists. Especially as their children grow older, they want to remove them from certain company and influences.

Sometimes connected with this emphasis, occasionally as a separate approach, we find an emphasis on evangelism. The school will be defended and promoted as a place where evangelism can take place. Sometimes this is seen as evangelism directed at the children of Christian parents. Alternatively, the admission policy will be made very open in order to attract a group of students from non-Christian backgrounds who can be evangelized.

While many of the schools which have this evangelistic emphasis produce and use curricula which are distinctive and individual, there are differences from the approach advocated here. One is that the way in which they reach a 'Christian' curriculum tends to be by the removal of what are regarded as highly objectionable items. Thus offensive novels and the teaching of evolution may be removed from the curriculum but otherwise it

[95]

is substantially the state school curriculum. Often the methodology will be dominated by ideas current in state schools, as for instance, the idea of the child teaching himself. Thus, rather than instituting inquiry into the roots of the approaches in state schools, certain individual objectionable things are changed.

Sometimes, especially when evangelism is the emphasis, there may be few changes from the state school approach and curriculum. The school may simply advertise itself as doing better what the state school does. It will point to higher academic standards.

Both these approaches, the sheltering approach and the evangelistic one, can lead to an emphasis on high school. It is at high school age that parents become concerned over issues like drugs and sexual promiscuity. Further, the teenager often seems a better target for evangelism.

Behind the concern for the sheltering of the child there is a basic conviction. It is that sin is primarily due to influences outside the child. Removing the child from these influences is the way to safeguard him.

If the curriculum and methodology are almost exactly the same as in the state school, then some other way must be found by which the truth of God comes through to the child. Often that is through some separate activity, such as special chapel services, assemblies, retreats, etc.

We have been talking in generalities but it is possible in these generalities to describe an approach which forms an alternative to the approach suggested in this book. In contrast to the emphasis here on curriculum and teaching method, there is an emphasis on school as an environment. It is a place where children are isolated from bad influences and are brought under influences emanating from God. There tends to be a concern with a tightly regulated environment. Sometimes this leads to extreme concern for uniformity of dress and behaviour. Emphasis falls primarily on high school age students and the sorts of problems they have.

A RESPONSE

It needs to be said at the outset that we do not reject out of hand the concerns of this group of Christian educators. We would not want to be seen as having no concern for the damage that is done when a child is presented with material beyond his moral and spiritual maturity level. We also have a concern for evangelism.

However we would like to see these Christian educators go further in being distinctively Christian and breaking with non-Christian education. In particular, with respect to their idea that sin is a matter of environment, we must differ from them. Scripture is specific that sin is in the heart of the child. Because it is in the heart, no environmental isolation will work. We must substitute the truth for what is in the heart. Hence distinctively Christian curricula are not a secondary consideration. They are a primary issue. It is probably no accident that many of these schools go along with the idea of the child teaching himself. If you do not see the sinful propensities of the child, then you can accept the idea that the child wants to learn and only needs to be given the materials.

How do we bring children to a knowledge of Christ? We saw in the first chapter that Scripture sees the parents as engaging in a constant, consistent course of example and instruction. We admit that it is hard to find an age at which childhood ends and adulthood begins. Nevertheless there can be problems if we take the sudden crisis model of adult conversion and try to impose it on children. The child may not yet clearly understand the terms and concepts we are using. We may confuse immaturity in faith with unbelief and discourage the child. Concluding that the child has not yet come to Christ we may not give the needed daily instruction in discipleship.

The scriptural approach treats the children of believers as part of the community of the people of God. It teaches them and yet it accepts them into the activities of the people of God. So we should follow the model in our school.

A further problem can arise when the sudden conversion model is applied not only to conversion but also to sanctification. Thus some people refrain from the daily training and discipline of children on the ground that they have yet to be sanctified or filled with the Spirit. Thus the child is denied what Scripture prescribes for him.

Our approach to the discipling of children should be the biblical one, namely, the constant daily presentation of truth and example. Hence our evangelism is not a matter of special speakers and chapels. It is a matter of daily classroom evangelism.

[97]

Certainly if we see evidence of a clear and deliberate rejection of the gospel we must confront the child with the seriousness of the situation and urge him to repent. Yet, especially with children, we need patience and wisdom to nurture them through the struggles of an immature faith and discipleship.

Thus the school is not a separate evangelistic agency. It is an extension of what the parents are already doing in discipling their children. From this follows our conviction that we do not concentrate on high school. We begin at infants' level and work right through the educational system. Not only does this give continuity. It is the practical approach. Pupils who transfer from state schools at high school age commonly bring with them serious academic and behavioural problems. Why spend so much time and effort in undoing the work of the state school? It is simpler to do it the right way from the beginning. There is an additional practical factor. A high school alone can be very expensive. An infants and primary school effectively subsidizes the high school.

NON-CHRISTIAN FAMILIES

So far we have talked in terms of Christian families. What happens when a non-Christian family wishes to send their children to a Christian school?

The school exists to help Christian parents to fulfil their obligations. That is its first priority. Yet sometimes, having done that, vacancies can be found.

Some would argue that the child from the non-Christian family simply 'does not belong'. Yet if non-Christian parents want to give their child the benefits of a Christian education, should we deny the child that benefit? Surely a Christian concern for the needs of that child motivates us to want to present him with the truth. If a church wanted to instruct its members in Scripture, would it object if an unbeliever wanted to come along and learn also? If one of the neighbourhood children wants to join you while you read the Bible and pray with your children, would you object? So the Christian school should have no objection if others also hear the truth.

However there are problems and special situations created by these non-Christian families and we need to develop policies to deal with them.

a) *Misconceptions*

The non-Christian will generally have little comprehension of a Christian school programme. He might expect nothing more than a formal devotional exercise to start the day. When he finds how pervasive the Christian approach is, and how it influences his child, he may withdraw him.

To meet this problem it is very important that we be honest. The non-Christian will be afraid his child is being sucked into something he did not anticipate. Let us warn them from the start. If we are honest with them, even if they do not understand the problem as we do, they will have less cause to fear us.

There is another reason for this honesty. We are not merely interested in the evangelization of children. Families need to be won to Christ. For non-Christian parents the contact with the school may be their first meaningful contact with Christianity. Let our walk before the parents be one which adorns the gospel of Christ. That involves sincerity and directness. It involves a genuine interest in ascertaining whether our school is the right school for their child.

That means spending time in talking to parents. We should not accept the notion of our culture that the raising of children is women's work and of no concern to the fathers. Whenever possible we should talk to both parents. That means a considerable load of interviewing. This should not all fall on the principal. It is a task that can easily be shared by parents.

Another area of possible misconception is the Christian policy of discipline. The parents should know this before they send their children to a Christian school.

b) *Maintaining Control*

The admittance of these non-Christian families raises a question of control. Are they to have a say in school policies? If a sizeable group of them demands such a say, then we risk losing the Christian character of the school.

It becomes therefore mandatory to have qualifications for becoming members of the controlling association. And non-Christian parents need to be informed about this from the outset. This does not mean that they will not attempt to join. Sometimes we have to make decisions which will not please everybody.

[99]

The prospect of such problems has discouraged some people from admitting children from non-Christian families. But the problems do not simply disappear if we restrict enrolment to Christian families, for some of the doctrines we have considered as very important for education are denied by people who would call themselves Christians and who may well be Christians in God's eyes. For example, some Christians teach that children are not really sinners until they reach an age that they call an age of accountability. Others would deny that God has elected men to salvation. Again we may find Christians trying to hold to both Christianity and evolution.

These beliefs have educational consequences of which many people are unaware. They may be attracted to a school by the practical results they see in pupils, yet doubt the beliefs which lie behind the programme. Initially that may not matter. Eventually it must lead to the appointment of board members and teachers whose beliefs are different from the beliefs of the school's founders, and who consequently accept various aspects of a non-Christian approach to education.

In other words, the educational direction of the school can be undermined by Christians as well as by non-Christians. That means that the school, if it wants to maintain its biblical direction, must set some standards of belief for entrance into the controlling association, and also for teachers. A convenient way of doing this is to adopt confessions that are specifically Reformed in teaching. They cover the crucial doctrines and exist in forms representing the major denominational groupings. The sections which enter into such matters as church government and the like are not directly relevant to the school. Thus there are the Three Forms of Unity (Heidelberg Catechism, Belgic Confession, and Canons of Dordt) for the Continental Reformed Churches, the Westminster Confession for Presbyterians, the Savoy Declaration for Congregationalists, the Old London (or Philadelphia) Confession for Baptists, and the Thirty-Nine Articles for Anglicans.

c) *Children with Problems*

Children with problems, from both Christian and non-Christian families, form a significant proportion of children enrolled in Christian schools. The reason is simple and obvious. It was the problem which first made the parents look for an alternative school. This problem may be somewhat lessened but it will not be removed by restricting enrolments to Christian families. Problems come also from those families.

These problems may be of an academic or a behavioural nature. Frequently the child has both problems.

We must be prepared for the dishonesty of parents in connection with problem children. Parents can become so desperate to find something for their child that they conceal the extent of the problem. They may make insincere professions of Christian faith in order to have the child placed.

Some schools seek to meet the problem by setting high academic standards for entry. While this weeds out many of the problem cases, it is most questionable as a practice for a Christian school. It excludes children from genuinely Christian families who perform poorly academically, but would be strongly supportive of the school, and admits academically bright children from nominal or non-Christian families. It excludes those whose poor performance is due to past poor schooling or who possess few skills in the academic area. As Christians we should not show indifference to the needs of these academically weaker students. In the compassion of Christ we are to reach out to the needy. As mentioned earlier, there may be physical disabilities so severe that the average Christian school lacks the facilities to cope with them. The commoner case, however, is poor academic performance with no obvious physical disability.

The adoption of a policy of willingness to admit the academically weaker student often creates problems for the school. Some portion of those problems may derive from problems in the home. Parents may live in a way which produces very disruptive consequences in their children. That can be true for Christian as well as non-Christian families, though obviously obedience to Christ is the best way to deal with the problems. When confronted with the problems in their own children they can make various responses. They may seek to change themselves. As part of the whole Christian community, the Christian school should do all it can to assist people in facing their problems. Alternatively they may refuse to change but look to others to solve their children's problems for them.

It is this latter situation which creates the greatest difficulty and misery for all. The problems will not be ultimately solved by the school because they are in the parents. In an age in which materialism, marital breakdown, sexual immorality, and violence are rampant, we can expect many such problems.

The child may be both victim and offender in this situation. As he makes his own sinful response to the parents' sin, so he complicates the problem.

What should the school do? First, it must be honest. If the problem is at least in part that of the parents, then they have to be told so. Persons who want a school which will just take care of their children, but not interfere in their private lives, should not choose a Christian school.

If the parents respond to this then we are on our way to solving not just a child's problem but a whole family problem. Once again, however, we must stress how important it is to reach fathers. There is a persistent, but quite false, idea that children's problems are in the wife's domain. She may also be partly victim and partly offender in a complex initiated by a husband's problems.

If the parents do not respond, the school faces a dilemma. It can be in a situation in which there is no hope of progress. Whatever it tries to do for the child is counteracted by the parents. The child is caught between the school's standards and the parents' standards. Just because the home is the primary institution, and the school a poor second, the home will most likely win. Yet the result is not inevitable, for the parents will be presenting a standard contrary to God's truth. By the work of the Spirit of God, the child may come to choose God's truth. That in itself will not resolve all problems. The parents may, when they see the child being influenced, withdraw the child from the school. If they do not, the child will be faced with the difficult calling of living as a Christian in a non-Chrisian home. He will need all the support and encouragement the school can give.

The other eventuality creates a much greater problem for the school. The child rejects the gospel and the standards presented by the school. All that the school does to try to change the attitude of the pupil is counteracted by the parents. If the problem is academic, the incentive the school gives to the pupil to make progress may be negated by the indifference of the home, its indifference to the discipline, rest, and routine that a child needs if he is to perform successfully. If the problem is behavioural, the parents may undermine attempts at discipline and training or confirm the child's negative view of himself, his work, and the school.

The school faces a difficult choice. The child will probably get worse in another school, or at least be withdrawn from the influences which would restrain him. Yet his presence in the school may be disruptive and detrimental to the whole school community. Sometimes parents will respond to the growing conflict between home and school by removing the child. Sometimes the school must make the decision by expelling the child. That is never a happy decision but we must face the fact that the school does not have the police powers of the state. It may discipline but it cannot ultimately coerce the rebellious pupil. If home and school work together, very great and serious problems can be overcome. Where home works against school and the child is in rebellion against God, the school cannot win.

With all these things in view, the initial interview becomes even more crucial. Very often the representatives of the school come to the interview and come away from it without a full knowledge of the situation. The tendency of parents to hide the real problems in order to have the child admitted has already been mentioned. There are several things a school can do. If the school makes its enrolment policy clear it may encourage openness in the parents. If they know that poor academic performance or lack of Christian profession will not automatically exclude the child, they may be more honest and open about the extent of the problem.

Further, the school should engage in some sort of academic testing in order to establish whether there is a problem. It is not always wise to rely upon reports and results from other schools. They can have low standards or be 'plain wrong'. Yet in using tests one must stress that the purpose is primarily to ascertain if there is a problem and to choose the appropriate class or remedial help, rather than to exclude pupils who do not perform well academically.

Having done all this, the school may yet face a problem. It cannot make dark insinuations about a problem when it does not know that one exists. All it can do is to lay out school policy. Primarily this involves co-operation between home and school. Parents who are frustrated by the lack of information from school, when they know there is a problem, will welcome this. Parents who want the school to deal with a problem they are causing will not welcome it. They may still persist in enrolling the child, but when the inevitable conflict comes, they should have no excuse. Once again honesty and directness, in the context of a genuine desire to help children with their problems, is the best approach.

Sometimes the problems are obvious. A divorce or separation is an obvious example. Once again we cannot assign blame when we do not have the facts. The one parent who brings the child to the school may or may not be partially or wholly to blame for the home breakdown. We must honestly present to the parent the fact that the child enters a school in which a family of husband and wife is taken as God's plan. To break that is sin. That does not mean an unwillingness to help children and families caught in the problem. It simply means that the school will not treat what is common in society as being what is normal and right.

Curriculum implications stem from this whole set of problems. We cannot assume that a child coming from a home full of problems will be eager to plunge into school work. Occasionally success at school will serve as an escape from the problem. More commonly the problem crowds out any interest in school work.

There is, therefore, a need for the personality of a teacher who can grab the child out of his absorption with his own problems and motivate him to work and achieve. A teacher who merely lends a hand to further what the child is already doing is of little use in this situation. What is needed is a teacher who will take centre stage and by word, personality, and example, communicate the truth and love the child needs. It was argued earlier that this is what the child with problems needs academically. It is also what he needs emotionally. Often he has been starved of interaction with a firm yet loving person.

Shyness or lack of concern in the teacher can hinder him from playing that leading role. Yet it must also be said that firmness and loudness are not all that is needed. The teacher of quiet personality may be just as effective. The crucial thing is that love is giving. The loving person projects his love and his concern. Projection of personality without love, or love without its conveyance to the child, are not what is needed, or what is required by the truth of God.

SHELTERING AND EXPOSURE

Sometimes Christian parents will reject the idea of having children from non-Christian families mingle with their children at school. That negates what they want the school to do, namely, to shelter their child.

Once again the issue here concerns the source of sin. Sin is in the heart of the child. That leads to several conclusions. The attempt to protect the child by excluding non-Christians is futile. It is not the exclusion of others that protects the child. It is the truth of God that counteracts the propensities of the sinful nature.

Knowing the propensities of the sinful nature of the child, we are concerned that the child should not be exposed to problems and temptations beyond his spiritual maturity level. Thus we do not agree with those who see sheltering as the solution to the sin problem in children. Nor do we agree that children should be indiscriminately exposed to temptation.

In practice this means that we do not exclude a child just because he might be a bad influence. Every child is potentially a bad influence. We would exclude a child who presented temptations beyond the maturity level of other children.

That policy also has a benefit for children from Christian homes. They are not attending a school where they might assume that they are Christians merely because everybody who attends the school is supposedly Christian. They are mixing with children from different backgrounds. Children from non-Christian homes may present problems, but they also have abilities, for they too are creatures made by God. The student from the Christian home can benefit from the stimulus and example of those abilities. Certainly problems arise, but they do so in a context where they can be dealt with from the Word of God by Christian teachers. We cannot claim that our schools will have no moral problems. We can claim that our policy is to deal with them in terms of God's Word. That in itself provides a very good example for children as they themselves learn to apply the Word of God to men.

৩ 8 ৩

History

There is no one area of the curriculum that is more basic than others. They relate to one another. The principles used in one area may well be applicable in another. Hence, there is no particular order in the presentation of the various subjects.

HISTORY AND CREATION

Superficially we might think that science is concerned with creation, history with what has happened since creation. Yet we cannot make so neat a division. The fact of creation changes our whole understanding of history. For example, an evolutionist can write a history of the development of the social institution of marriage. It will, of course, be a branch of fiction but he will nevertheless, in all seriousness, write a history of how man evolved from the promiscuity of animal relationships to legal marriage. In turn that will influence his writing of later history because he will see marriage as something that happened to evolve and that has no particular claim to be a permanent institution.

What we touch upon here is the fact that creation was not merely finished with respect to the stars or the animals. It was finished in respect to man. Man had instituted for him things like marriage and labour as creation ordinances. Thus there are things that will not change while the old creation remains.

History is about change and about passing judgment on those changes. For the non-Christian it can become change from absolute flux to absolute flux. This changed, so what? Somebody tried to change that, so what? Creation gives you a fixed starting point. You know some things that should not change.

There is a second very important thing which we learn not just from the mere fact of creation but from the biblical account of creation. That is, that there are very few of what could be called 'creation ordinances', that is, things ordained by God at the beginning of human social existence. The traditional list is Sabbath-keeping, work, and marriage.

The crucial fact about many societies is that they try to expand that list. Of course they do not (or very rarely) appeal to the biblical account of creation as justification. Yet what they are trying to do is to expand the list of things that have the sanctity and authority of creation ordinances. Tribal societies commonly place the origin of their social structures back in the time of beginnings. The pagan cultures like the Sumerian, in Bible times, did that also. The result is that such societies find it hard to write histories of human society. The significant thing about the Bible is that it contains elements of a history of human society. Genesis 4 describes the origin of institutions such as the city and life-styles such as nomadic herding. When we investigate and discuss the origins of social institutions, ways of life, etc., we are following that biblical example. As explained later, the non-Christian often does not have the same interest in changes in human society.

THE ACTS OF MAN

There is a second way in which belief in creation changes our understanding of history. We know God created a good world. We know God created man good. But he is no longer good. History is the study of the acts of man. We bring to it a basis of judgment in God's Word. Every human choice is a moral choice. That is, it will be done out of obedience to God's commands or it is disobedience. There is a lot of opposition to seeing history in those terms, so we should examine the point more closely.

One of the consequences of naturalistic and evolutionary thinking is to see man as the product of his environment. Man, it is claimed, is a creature of the pressures and forces which come to bear on him. Man cannot be expected to do anything but what he is compelled to do by his circumstances. That view of man is contrary to the whole biblical presentation of man as responsible to obey God, no matter what the pressures on him. It is very helpful to study the way in which the biblical historians present their characters. They see them as responsible before God. Take the story of King Saul. The text very clearly tells us that Saul does certain things because of the pressure of circumstances. He offers sacrifice because Samuel does not arrive as expected. He saves the Amalekite cattle to please the people following him. To the mind of many non-Christians the existence of circumstances, pressuring in a certain direction, explains and excuses Saul's action. The biblical historians are aware of the pressures on man. But there is another way in which it is possible for man to go. That is to resist the pressures in obedience to God. Man is not a mere victim of circumstances. He makes a choice for or against God.

If we view man merely as a creature held in bondage to his circumstances, his history becomes little more than the story of the pressures and circumstances. Of course we are interested as Christians in that, in order to know the choices being placed before men in the past. Nevertheless they are not all there is to history. There is still the human choice.

LEADERSHIP AND SOCIETY

A further consequence of seeing man as nothing more than a product of his environment is that the leader has no significance in human history and human society. The leader will also be the product of the circumstances of his time. His actions and decisions, and the reasons behind them, will have no particular significance for the study of history. Of course we would recognize that leaders often do give in to the pressures of the time but that is not necessarily the case. The individual decision of a man can be significant.

This denial of the significance of human actions or human leadership is one of the factors in the common replacement of history in school curricula by sociology. This sociology assumes that the significant factor is the social mass acting according to some social law. Its object is to investigate social groups in the past and see how they conform to the same laws as social groups today.

Sociology is not wrong in itself, but the assumptions commonly built into it, which deny the significance of individual human action in history, have to be resisted. If history is the mere outworking of social laws which determine what the mass of people will do, then there is no possibility of a distinctive Christian presence in this present age, because the social laws will make us conform, as they have made people in the past conform. It also takes out of history that personal and individual element which is part of the fascination of history to the average student.

HISTORY AND HUMAN INSTITUTIONS

We must go back to Genesis 4 because there is one other significant thing to be drawn from it. We read here of the development of new institutions or life-styles: the city, nomadic pastoralism, metallurgy (note, bronze and iron working originate together: there is not a Bronze Age followed by an Iron Age), polygamy. Not every development is good. Polygamy certainly was not. Not every development was bad in itself. The city, pastoral nomadism, music, metallurgy all came to be practised by God's people. Yet no development was mandatory, even the ones which are not wrong. There is no biblical requirement that you live in a city, but you may do so. There is no biblical requirement that you be a nomadic pastoralist, but you may be one.

THE WHIG VIEW OF HISTORY

So we see here that development of new life-styles may be right or may be wrong, but those life-styles cannot be mandatory. Unless we know this we shall never escape one of the most important traps in contemporary approaches to history. This trap begins with the widespread assumption that the modern European life-style, especially the British style or American style with its political liberalism, material affluence, etc., is better than any other lifestyle: not just materially better but morally better. History is then written as the story of the progress towards this state. Persons who aided that development are good. Persons who opposed that development are bad. Today this is commonly called 'the Whig view of history'.

Along with this theory goes the belief that what is modern is intrinsically good. To oppose it is to be morally wrong. It was pointed out earlier how tribal societies, by expanding the number of creation ordinances, effectively prevent development or at least prevent a consciousness of development. The Whig view of history effectively reverses that, placing the normative social forms at the end of history rather than at the beginning of history. Whatever is modern comes to have the authority of a creation ordinance. Any retrogression to an earlier institution must be condemned.

There are many today who would condemn this Whig view of history as quite wrong in every respect. They would blame the ecological crisis on the view of progress which lies behind it. As Christians we cannot simply condemn it. Nor can we approve it. Here lies the trap. The idea of progress arises in part from a secularization of the Christian hope. As the believer looks hopefully to the future with the coming of Christ, so the unbeliever has looked with hope to the coming kingdom of man. Because the structure is the same, though man has been put in God's place, many Christians have sadly come to accept that what seems to be progress is necessarily good. Whatever appears as new in Western societal institutions must be good. On the other hand, many of the heroes in the Whig view of history were Christians: the Reformers, the Puritans, Wilberforce, etc. Behind the rejection of the Whig view of history there lies in part an antipathy to Christians of their type. And yet the Whig view of history did not do justice to such men. They were not intending to create a liberal secular state.

What is wrong with the Whig view of history is that it assumed that progress towards what we now have is good, instead of judging what we now have by biblical standards. Not only did that view declare to be good some things that were bad, but it also made mandatory some things that are merely permissible. Let me pluck an example out of the air. Is the development of the modern political party and the idea of government and opposition good? We have tended to assume that it is and have promoted its development in places like Africa where the results can be bad when the parties coincide with tribal divisions.

HISTORICISM

I have spoken of a rejection of Whig history. The rejection has come largely from the school which is called historicism and which is a branch of romanticism. Historicism is an attempt to study each historical period on its own merits, on its own terms and not as a prelude to some later and more advanced period. It stresses feeling, intuition, and empathy rather than reason. The historian has to feel his way into each historical period. Romanticism has been called 'spilt religion'. It is German pietism with God removed but a feeling left. So one has sympathy with the feeling or mood of a period. One feels in tune with it rather than assessing it in a critical way.

Romanticism also has a dislike for analysis, for breaking things down into parts by analysis. It likes wholes. Organic unity is a catch-phrase of romanticism. So countries are an organic whole. History should feel its way into countries at various periods, not analysing for trends but seeking empathetic understanding. One strange consequence is that history becomes the history of the foreign relations of a country. You must not look at internal relations because that denies the organic unity of the country. Rather you study the country in its external manifestations. The idea of national temperaments is akin to this.

Even though historicism aims at historical understanding it easily becomes anti-historical and 'plain dangerous'. Where one cannot analyse, it becomes very hard to see developing trends. There is also no criticism since it is a matter of feeling sympathy. Hence there is no subjecting a period to the test of God's Word. Historicists tend to treat countries as a whole. You finally reach the conclusion that nations are able to do no wrong. Their pursuit of their own particular national spirit is above criticism. The Nazi movement with its belief in German national identity has elements of historicism. Hence the description of it as dangerous.

Romanticism has not been so influential on Anglo-Saxon historiography as on German historiography. You can see traces. For example, some courses do not seek to understand the historical development of the Middle Ages. They ask rather: What did it feel like to live at that time? The mystical aspects of medieval religion are highlighted. (Romanticism is pro-Middle Ages and anti-Reformation because it likes religion of mystical feeling, setting doctrine aside). There is no criticism of the actions of people in the period; there is no study of the Middle Ages as a developing, changing phenomenon. By the time it gets down to school level, that approach merges with another approach which stems from making man a creature of his environment, and is concerned solely with the physical aspects of life. What did people eat? What did they wear? There is nothing wrong in itself in studying how people felt in a particular age; and in investigating the physical circumstances of their lives. But the historian should not stop there. These circumstances are the environment in which people make decisions. The decisions as well as the environment must be evaluated.

THE PROVIDENCE OF GOD

So far we have not dealt with a matter high on the list of topics to consider in a biblical approach to history, namely, the providence of God. Judgments on human actions were considered first because there are certain unbiblical understandings of providence which exclude the possibility of passing judgment on human actions. As we shall consider in more detail when we come to science, God's providence became misunderstood as a fixed and unchangeable set of laws. (For example, think of the consequences of saying that every law-breaker, whether he breaks civil law or God's law, is driven on by certain psychological forces which have arisen within him by the operation of fixed physical laws over which he has no control. You end up with no possibility of guilt or responsibility.) That notion of the world as a fixed order of laws becomes confused with or justified by the Christian idea of providence. The result is the idea of progress already mentioned. Whatever happens in the course of Western development is God's will and must not be subject to criticism. Paradoxically a moral judgment is yet brought in; persons who want to halt or reverse the course of progress are wrong. But if everything is providentially ordered then reversion must also be divinely ordained and all persons who oppose a reversion, once under way, are opposing God.

To escape this confusion it is imperative to look at what the Bible says, not in one or two aspects only but in its entirety. God has revealed a law for man to follow. If he does not follow that law he is responsible and may be justly criticized. At the same time God also uses all human acts, including sinful acts, to fulfil his purposes. To take a few examples: the crucifixion of Christ was the greatest crime of human history, yet it was the central part of God's plan. Joseph said to his brothers, about their selling him into slavery: 'You meant it for evil, but God meant it for good.' God ordains all things, yet man is responsible when he breaks God's law. If you do not hold on to both those truths you are in great trouble.

Hence it is not a denial of God's providence to criticize or to seek to reverse developments in Western history. Whole social structures and social trends may be wrong. The purpose of the study of history is not to discern where events are leading so that we can go with them. It is to subject the trend of events to the criticism of God's revealed law. (We could comment in passing that the debate between Whig history and historicism is parallel to the debate between technology and the environment. That debate sets progress, understood as Western material, technological progress, over against a romantic feeling for nature.)

There is therefore a call for subjecting human acts to criticism and also for trying to discern the pattern in God's providential ordering of human acts. The Books of Kings are engaged in doing this very thing. They explore such questions as: Why was Jehu's line allowed to continue on the throne of Israel for four generations though he was an idolater? Why was Jerusalem destroyed so soon after the reign of the good Josiah? We should not claim that our understanding of providence has any infallibility but if we think biblically, surely we must attain to a measure of understanding.

HISTORY AS EXAMPLE

It used to be traditional in Australian primary schools to learn about the early explorers of Australia. Some people still cannot imagine Australian history without the explorers. Why were they chosen to form the core of primary Australian history? One doubts if the generation raised on the explorers knew why they studied them. Perhaps even the teachers did not know why they were in the state curriculum.

It came from a conviction that history is about the great men of the past. We study the great men so that they may be an example to us. The purpose of the study of history is moral example. Australian history is rather lacking in great men so the explorers were chosen for want of something better.

It would be hard to find as clear a tradition in the teaching of Australian history today. One prominent trend forms an interesting contrast. It is to study the individual settler, especially the physical conditions of his life. This is a reaction against the older view of the purpose of history. It is no longer the great men that are studied. It is the little men. For the premise is that the so-called 'great men' did not determine the course of history. Today many fail to see any purpose or direction in history. All that is important is what the individual experiences. So the only matters of importance in early

Australia were the physical experiences of the individual settler.

Both this exaltation of the 'great men' and this opposing treatment of the 'little men' rest upon metaphysical assumptions. Those assumptions are rarely made explicit. They are part of the hidden curriculum. If they were made explicit there would be endless arguments about the assumptions on which the curriculum rests. They remain hidden to both teachers and pupils who do not see any real point in what they are studying.

A second major reason for the study of the 'little men' is environmental determinism. That is, a belief that men are the products of their environment leads to the conclusion that the harsh physical circumstances of Australia are what has shaped the national life.

ENVIRONMENT, PEOPLE AND LEADER

Are we against teaching about early settlers and explorers? Certainly not! However we must teach those subjects in a way consistent with our Christian profession. Are men merely heroes? Are they always positive examples? The explorers cannot just be taught as positive examples. Many were vain and foolish. Our view of the sinfulness of man must determine the way we teach history.

Similarly we cannot adopt the attitude that the actions of leaders are only the result of the sum of the actions of individual settlers. It is interesting to look at the treatment of Jeroboam I by the biblical historians. The rebellion against Rehoboam, the son of Solomon, was sparked off by the people as a whole. Jeroboam was in Egypt when it got under way. In that sense Jeroboam was no more than a spokesman for the people in the revolt (I Kings 12:1–3). Yet once he was established as king he did things on his own initiative and this in turn affected the people. He led Israel into the sin of worshipping the calves at Dan and Bethel and the biblical description of him is 'the man who made Israel sin' (2 Kings 10:29). Who determines the course of history? Is it the people or the environment so that the leader is a mere puppet? Clearly it was not so in the case of Jeroboam. Is it the great man? Are the people merely being swayed by leaders? Clearly not in the case of the rebellion of Israel!

This is really very simple. History is an interaction of leaders, environment and people, where people make real decisions; they

[114]

are often wrong, but are decisions nevertheless. Yet are the text-books teaching it that way? Often they are not because their meta-physical assumptions do not allow them to look at the real world.

HISTORY IN ISOLATION

What was happening in Australia during the era of exploration and of settlement? Were people running ahead of the leaders? Clearly the squatters were ahead of them. What was wrong with the leadership? Can that question be answered without looking at the ideas of land ownership and class structure brought from England? In other words, can you write a true Australian history merely by taking selectors and squatters in isolation? It is simple common sense that Australian history cannot be understood in isolation. Yet that is what we see in so many textbooks and not just in Australian history. You find also this or that aspect of British or American history selected to be studied in isolation. The very structure of history requires continuity. It requires that we understand what went before in order to understand what came after. Why do people defy common sense?

TEACHING AND COMPLEXITY

Once again, one must look for the philosophical roots of the method suggested here for understanding history – that we look for the interaction of leadership and the group led, that we assess the rightness or wrongness of human action, that we see how ideas and institutions, inherited from a previous time, influence man's action in this time – all of that creates a complex model of writing history. It can be simplified. Its main points can be conveyed to students. It can be taught but – here is the rub – it must be taught. And teaching is anathema today. The teacher is merely a resource person while the child teaches himself.

Thus what was said earlier against romanticism is relevant, not only in rejecting the particular romanticist (or historicist) view of history. It has relevance for all that we teach in history. If the complex, yet fascinating, nature of the web of historical events is to be revealed to the child the teacher has to take the lead. Once the pupil has seen the way history is to be analysed, and has matured in his analytical skills, then he can write history for himself.

[115]

BUILDING THE HISTORICAL SENSE

It was pointed out earlier that Dewey's whole position depended upon asserting that the child is fundamentally uninterested in anything outside his immediate world. He is interested in the past only for its relevance to the present. This conviction, however false it may be about the child, has led to the general extinction of history in the lower grades. It has contributed to a tendency to replace history by politics or sociology. It is the contemporary institutions and society which are studied, not their historical roots.

Actually the child may be fascinated by stories of former places and events. What he lacks is a framework within which to place these events. One of our first tasks in the primary school is to build that framework. Certainly that can be done by incorporating stories which interest; stories which encourage him to begin developing his ability to judge historical events by the light of Scripture; stories which show men struggling to do what is right in difficult circumstances. Nevertheless we want more than interesting and uplifting stories. We want a framework of history, a time sense to develop.

Why is this important? It is important because the child has to be able to connect where he is in time and in the purposes of God to the framework for world history given in Scripture. He has ultimately to see the story of man's rebellion against God in its original, later, and contemporary phases and to recognize, in contrast to that, the work of the grace of God, bringing men back to the Father.

This view leads away from the very technical and atomizing approach that one sometimes sees. That approach arises from a denial of any real over-all purpose and movement in history. It sees the purpose of the subject of history as being the teaching of a technique of analysis. Where the analysis is applied is really rather unimportant. One might as well teach thirteenth-century Mongolian history rather than the history of the Renaissance and Reformation; or one decade in an obscure Hampshire village in the seventeenth century rather than the French Revolution and the Napoleonic Wars.

This is not to say that it is wrong to study detail. It is not an argument against an in-depth case study, but a contention that these details have to be put within a larger context.

Both in Australian and American history there has been a tendency to divorce the particular national history from its continuity with European, African, and Asian history. Great detail is taught in the national history but that national history is taught without its European background. Do those who know the story of the Pilgrim Fathers know anything of the ecclesiastical dispute in England that motivated the migration? Do those who have heard about the transportation of convicts to Australia understand the legal and social theory that lay behind the policy? Do those who deplore what was done to the native peoples in both cases, and to the African slaves, know anything of the beliefs about man, civilization, and land ownership which were used in justification?

Very often these things are ignored or taught most superficially. A denial of the possibility of truth and a belief in environmental determinism leads to a depreciation of the importance of ideas and ideology. Thus we see Australian and American history as though the convicts or the Revolutionary War made a complete break with the past. The heritage of ideas and institutions is ignored.

PATTERNS IN HISTORY

We want to be able to study the decisions of man in the context of his beliefs and institutions. If we do that, do we find patterns to history? If by patterns we mean cycles that always recur in a fixed order, if we mean that we can always predict the result of an action, then we are deceiving ourselves. One of the reasons is investigated by the biblical historians. It is the combination of longsuffering and kindness with justice and wrath in the character of God. The biblical historians supply us with examples of this: Rehoboam remained on the throne of Judah, not because of his righteousness but because of God's mercy and promise to David (1 Kings 11:34); Jehu was promised that his sons to the fourth generation would sit upon his throne because he had executed God's wrath against the house of Ahab, and that, even though he was an idolater (2 Kings 10:29–31); Josiah's sons were to be removed from the throne, despite the goodness of Josiah, because the Lord would not turn from his fierce wrath against Manasseh (2 Kings 23:26, 27).

The cases of Jehu and Josiah bring the whole matter into sharp focus. Jehu's descendants to the fourth generation came to the throne. In contrast, during the reign of Josiah's sons, the kingdom of Judah was destroyed. Yet of them all, the fathers and the descendants, only Josiah followed the Lord with all his heart. If it was pure abstract logic you would expect Josiah's descendants to continue longer than Jehu's. But the combination of longsuffering and wrath in a personal God does not lead to pure predictability. History cannot be written in that way. Hence the rationalist, whose premise is that either you have total order, logic, and predictability, or you have chaos, looks at history as chaos.

We can, nevertheless, see a pattern. We can predict what, unless God in his mercy intervenes, will be the consequence of an action. The biblical historians are concerned to see the results of actions. If you read the books of Samuel or Judges you will see that very often the authors do not interrupt the flow of the narrative to tell you whether a certain action was right or wrong. Yet the average reader of the Bible can tell you if it was right. How does he do it? It is because the story is told in such a way as to show the consequences of those actions. Good actions lead to blessing; evil ones to disaster.

The romantic approach by isolating a particular period, the approach of saying that only modern, modern, modern history is significant; some forms of thematic approach where history is made incidental to the theme – all of these do not give you sufficient scope to see the consequences for good or ill of ideas and institutions. Consequently they make history irrelevant. They turn us aside from any possibility of learning anything for good or ill from history, and of seeing the historical roots of our present day blessings and problems.

We can summarize what we should be studying in history in the following way. We should be studying the actions of man against the background of the environment that in actuality, or perhaps in his own mind, limits or influences his decisions. That background, of course, includes his beliefs and institutions. We are subjecting those actions to judgment both by comparing them to biblical standards and by studying their consequences. In undertaking such a study we are confronted again and again with mystery; the mystery which lies in the actions of a personal God. Our study is with a view to seeing what the consequences are of human decisions and searching for the roots of our own situation, so that we may know how and what to change.

That understanding of the subject leads us to consider the big topics and the bigger time spans. It leads away from the atomizing approach. It leads to a sense of world history.

HISTORY AND SOCIAL STUDIES

One of the consequences of seeing man as a mere product of his environment is to make the study of the environment especially important. If there is no significant human decision, then we can only understand history by a study of the environment which produces the decision. That line of thought leads naturally to a closer connection of history and geography.

It leads also to the conclusion that the geography is more important than the history. For the geography is more basic. It is the cause. Historical actions are the result. Hence we have seen social studies courses which tend to be really courses in human geography with very little attention given to history.

If we are to be true to Scripture we must affirm that people make real choices. Environment places a choice before people. The Israelites as they came out of Egypt were faced with a difficult environment. Yet we cannot say it was the environment which caused them to grumble against God and put him to the test. That came from their hearts.

We need to know the environment to understand the choices placed before people. Unless we know the circumstances, we cannot know whether the choice was an easy or a difficult one. Hence geography is very important to the study of history. Yet it is not the basis of history.

There is a simple fact which refutes environmental determinism, namely, that human ideas and institutions are transported from one country to another. Certainly they may be modified in the new environment but they still survive. Often they survive when quite inappropriate to the new environment. Once again we need the study of geography in order to make this tendency clear to pupils. To understand man in a particular period we need to know both his geographical context and the historical tradition he brings to that context. Once again it needs to be stressed that we should not study American and Australian history apart from the roots of those cultures.

If as Christians we are to understand our present age we must understand the contemporary environment and the legacy which

[119]

we bring from the past to that environment. The institutions and traditions which concern us have often developed in a geographical environment different from the one in which they are now being expressed. Hence it is hard to study the geography and history of a region together. It often makes more sense to develop the initial knowledge of them separately and then to bring that knowledge together.

HISTORY AND SOCIOLOGY/POLITICS/CIVICS

It used to be the case that people defended the value of historical study. Sometimes, as we have seen, they pointed to historical figures as moral examples. Sometimes they argued that understanding the historical roots of our present problems would enable us to solve them. We have seen the various tendencies today to move away from an interest in history. There has also been a tendency to substitute for it other disciplines. These disciplines tend, especially on a school level, to be without a historical perspective. Thus children may study contemporary society or contemporary political structures.

The rationale for doing this is very similar to the reason that used to be given for the study of history. It is that people need to understand contemporary society and political structures in order to be able to function in today's world. In theory that is unobjectionable. In practice it produces some major problems.

These problems relate to the ways in which these studies of the present world are and are not relativistic. Suppose school children are asked to do a sociological survey of their neighbourhood to discover what proportion of the adults have been divorced. The conclusion would probably be that divorce is a relatively common phenomenon. That information tends to incline people to the conclusion there is nothing wrong with divorce. Thus this sociological study has a relativistic tendency. It tends to the conclusion that there are no absolutes in the area of marital faithfulness. Now, of course, the data on the frequency of divorce does not logically lead to that conclusion. It is rather the impression people derive when that really distressing data is treated without any moral or even emotional framework.

Suppose children were asked to do a study of political party trends in a number of recent elections. It is the sort of thing that students of politics do regularly. Yet it also has a consequence. If the data is presented without any critical framework, then one tends to the conclusion that the party political system is normal and right.

In short the tendency of these forms of contemporary study is towards an acceptance of the practices and structures of contemporary society. This is in spite of the fact that these studies are justified on the ground that they will help to make our world better. As a matter of fact, unless there is a basis of judgment, the tendency will be to confirm the present structures. That tendency to confirm the present structures in turn tends to weaken the basis of criticism. For example, the more we tend to accept divorce as normal, the more we undermine any authority for the Bible. Thus these studies are relativistic in the sense that they relativize the moral basis of criticism. On the other hand they have an absolutizing tendency. They tend to give absolute validity to contemporary practice.

If history is taught with the Whig view of history, it will also absolutize contemporary practice because what is newest is regarded as being better. But history, properly taught, has the opposite tendency. It shows that things were once done in a different way. It exposes the often dubious bases on which contemporary practices developed. This tends to undermine the validity of contemporary practice. Thus history also has a relativizing tendency, but the opposite one to contemporary studies.

There are some who would advocate doing contemporary studies without a historical dimension but with a Christian critique. That is better than doing it without any critique. It still lacks a certain depth or dimension. Often, knowing how something originated helps us find a better alternative.

If we use history properly we shall be kept from absolutizing the past. For we must apply to men in the past the same sort of judgments we apply to contemporary society.

Obviously anybody who is clinging to an aspect of contemporary society or life which is contrary to Scripture does not want this sort of critical study. He will much prefer the pseudo-criticism of contemporary studies to real critical studies.

THE USE OF HISTORY

Some of the uses of history have been touched upon already. Deuteronomy is very much concerned with the use of Israel's past.

It serves as a reminder of God's power and faithfulness (7:17–19). The memory of past trials and humblings should keep Israel from pride when blessing comes (8:2–16). The memory of past failures should also serve to lessen pride (9:4–29). We should make such use of history in our day. Following this pattern would turn us from the proud man-centred studies of the national heroes of the past which so dominate many curricula.

∾ 9 ∾

Science

The previous chapter on history began not with the biblical doctrine of providence, but with creation. This chapter begins not with creation, but with providence. We need to get rid of the idea that the issue is creation and evolution. Certainly that is an important issue; but it is only one phase of the battle. Many Christian institutions initially opposed to evolution have succumbed to evolution, partly because they conceded the battle on more fundamental issues in understanding the relation between God and the creation.

GOD'S COVENANT WITH CREATION

The relationship between God and creation is a covenantal relationship. That applies, not just for the human or even the animate creation; it applies to the whole creation. It is the relation between the Lord who speaks commands and a creature who obeys the commands. That covenantal aspect applies from the very beginning. It is by word of command that the creation is brought into being. Further, there are individual commands addressed to different portions of his creation, because God's relation with creation is immediate. (We will return to this later.)

How does this affect our understanding of providence? God's relation to his creatures is still covenantal. He has a covenant with the sun and the moon, the day and the night (Jeremiah 31:35–37, 33:19–26). He commands his creatures, or permits his servants to command them and they obey (Psalms 33:6–9; 148:5, 6, 8; Amos 5:8; Isaiah 45:12; Numbers 20:8; Joshua 10:12–14; Isaiah 48:13; Matthew 8:26–27). If you look at those passages, you will see certain consequences. God's command, in accord with his longsuffering and goodness to man, maintains the regular operations of the creation. Day and night continue in obedience to his word. However, there is, in God, not only longsuffering and mercy. He is also the God of wrath and justice. Accordingly, his commands may bring about a change in the order which has been maintained during the period of longsuffering (Psalms 50:3, 4; 104:6–9; Amos 5:8).

GOD'S IMMEDIATE RELATIONSHIP WITH CREATION

It is because God speaks to the sun and moon his commands that the relationship between God and his creation is immediate. He does not have to go through some celestial switchboard which directs or perhaps mediates his commands to creation. Why make that point? The Greek concept of the world divided reality into two realms: an eternal realm of order and a realm of chaos. The order was partly implanted in the chaos, but was originally and conceptually distinct.

THE NON-CHRISTIAN VIEW OF NATURAL LAW

This was imported into Christendom with God placed above the order and made to be its Creator. Thus we have a threefold division: God, realm of order, world. The way in which God was held to relate to the world of order was ambiguous. Sometimes it was taught that God had created this realm at the beginning as something separate from himself; sometimes that the realm of order was simply the mind of God. There were consequences. If this realm of order was originally created by God to rule the creation, then it effectively stands between him and the particular parts of creation. God can contact creation only through this realm of order, and in effect he cannot contact it or act upon it because that would violate the realm of order. It would change the order, and bound up with the very notion of order in Greek thought was unchangeability. Hence, the order could not be changed. It also gave people problems with Genesis 1, because Genesis 1 does not report the creation first of this realm of order. If one held that the realm of order was actually the mind of God, then a knowledge of order leads one into the mind of God. Depending on the particular branch of Greek thought in the ascendancy, the order could have a strongly mathematical or strongly aesthetic colouring, or both. Hence came mysticisms. It is by contemplating the mathematical order, or the realm of beauty, or the beauty of mathematics that one comes into personal and intimate contact with God. Often the idea of the order as separate, and the idea of the order as part of the mind of God, were both held because the dominant philosophical influence was Neo-Platonism. Neo-Platonism sees the world as a series of less and less ordered emanations from the being of God, so the order is both God and a separate projection from God.

The originators of early modern science interpreted what they were discovering in terms of this framework. The order which they found in creation was based on the laws which God had originally given to rule the world (see T. S. Kuhn, *The Copernican Revolution*) and very soon they began to experience the consequences of that belief. If the laws of planetary or physical motion were the eternal laws of God, then they could not be changed. Immediately, miracles or any interventions of God in the world were excluded. God became shut out of his world by his own laws. The only purpose for God was as the original Creator of the world and its laws. This is the movement called deism. Further, having knowledge of God through his laws, men no longer needed revelation. Indeed, the miraculous character of revelation made it suspect.

THE GOD OF THE GAPS

When the implications of this belief became more obvious to Christians they fell back on the defence that there were certain areas that remained subject to God's intervention. 'Yes,' it was conceded, 'the motions of the heavens are immutable according to God's fixed laws, but there are areas like the development of species which are a result of God's direct intervention.' Hence we come into the 'god of the gaps' debate, with Christians trying to find room for divine activity in some areas while conceding that God was excluded from others by his own laws. Others were trying to carry through the deist world-view with greater consistency. That is, they attempted to find regularity, i.e., laws, in all areas. A God excluded from the world by his own law order was of very little practical consequence, except as a logical first cause. Hence, the idea of God became less and less important. The debate over uniformitarianism in geology and the origin of species has to be seen against this background. It was to complete the view of the world where God was not present, except as a first cause.

A BIBLICAL VIEW OF GOD AND THE WORLD

It is useless to be against evolution, but still to think in terms of the mechanistic universe. The logic of your position will under-cut your view of creation. The biblical God speaks directly to his creation, and the individual parts of it, to bring it into being, and again at particular times to his creatures. In that sense, creation and providence are linked together.

When you explore the purpose of this speaking you see that it creates and maintains a world fit for man, or, in judgment, it destroys that world. In the creating and maintaining we have the basis for human science. God prepares the world for man. Notice how in Genesis 1 the world is progressively developed to be suitable for man. Similarly the regularity of day and night, summer and winter, seedtime and harvest (Genesis 8:22) allows man to continue his regular life on the earth.

We must avoid a confusion between our human description of this regularity and the actual command which God addresses to the creation. Suppose a factory owner who manufactured cloth-ing employed an agent to buy wool for him. When the weather was cold, the factory used more wool to make warmer clothing. In summer the need for wool diminished. Each week the factory owner told the agent how much wool to buy. Soon those at the wool market could predict the size of the agent's purchase from the weather. They might even be able to write a mathematical equation to relate temperature and weight of wool. They might deduce that there was some 'law' inherent in the agent which caused this relationship. Yet could they get the agent to buy wool by merely quoting the 'law' they had deduced? Clearly not, for the agent would obey only his employer's commands. The law which the men at the wool market had deduced and the em-ployer's commands are not the same. The deduced 'law' does not allow for a change by the employer, for example, beginning to export clothing to the opposite hemisphere, or closing the factory entirely.

Taking over the distinction of this illustration into the question before us we ask, Is a so-called 'scientific law' our description of the regularity which God's commands preserve, or is it the command which God actually addresses to the creation? Obviously it is our description of the regularity. Try saying e = mc² and see if anything happens! Further, the Scripture affirms that man does not know God's commands to his creation. In rebuking Job's desire to be in the place of God and understand the full mystery of the universe, God says, 'Can you bind the beautiful Pleiades? Can you loose the cords of Orion? Can you bring forth the constellations in their seasons or lead out the Bear with its cubs? Do you know the laws of the heavens? Can you set up God's dominion over the earth? Can you raise your voice to the clouds and cover yourself with a flood of water? Do you send the lightning bolts on their way? Do they report to you, "Here we are"?' (Job 38:31–35). Notice the connection between knowledge of the commandment and the ability to command the rain. That connection has to be there because the command that God addresses to the creation is a powerful command. As was said previously, under the influence of Neo-Platonism these commands had become somewhat divorced from God, and hence were seen as intellectual concepts. In that framework of thought, to deny the possibility of knowing these concepts is tantamount to denying that God is Creator. But we do not have such problems. There is no intermediate thing between God and creation that keeps God out of his world.

The consequences of following the biblical view are clear. You do not have a problem with miracles. God in judgment may change his commands. Whereas he has commanded the seas to keep within their bounds (Psalm 104:6–9), he may in judgment call for the seas and pour them out on the land (Amos 5:8). Miracles are not a transgression of God's law for creation, because God's law does not exist as something outside of himself and independent of him. Rather it is the expression of his personal will, a will that combines longsuffering and wrath. Similarly, he can in mercy address special commands to his creatures as Christ did in his healing miracles.

CREATION

We turn now from this examination of how God rules the creation to the creation itself. God created in a series of distinct acts. Hence, the separateness of various aspects of creation. Plants and animals are separate. Even within each separate domain of the living creation, there are further distinctions. The plants and animals are created to reproduce after their kinds. Thus, we have a set of distinctions within creation because of God's separate acts of creation.

However, we have connections and likenesses that result from the way God created. He forms the creatures out of the ground. Thus there is a resemblance in the basic constituency of the different creatures, including man. It is important to stress this, for the controversy about evolution has tended to its minimization. In opposition to evolution, Christians have tended to stress the distinctiveness of the different animal groups. The evolutionist, working on the principle that all living creatures are evolved from the one original or at most from a few sources, has partly assumed and partly attempted to prove the biochemical unity of all of life. Probably the real situation is more complex than either party has thought. Given the common source material and common Creator, there is much biochemical and physiological unity. However, there is also evidence, not emphasized within an evolutionary environment, of fundamental differences in biochemical systems. We may well find similarities, but similarities which refuse to conform to the larger groupings postulated by the evolutionist.

Our teaching has to do justice both to the unity of biological nature flowing from the common origins we have mentioned, and the disunity flowing from God's separate creation and separate purpose for different parts of the biological world.

Talking about the purpose of creation, and especially of the animate creation, brings into focus the whole question of the relation of the animals to man. It is clear from Genesis 1 that the creation has its culmination with man; that he is its covenant lord. The world is created as a world suitable for man to live in and utilize. Against that background, we should not be happy with the distinction between pure and applied science. The unbeliever makes that distinction because he has no reason to expect that his exploration of the world will turn out to be useful. He hopes it will. He has no reason to believe it will. It is a happy accident that it turns out so. We, on the contrary, know why it is so.

CREATURES BESIDES MAN

However, the fact that the creation was made for man does not mean that man is the only creature for which it was made. There are other creatures who act as covenant lords and utilize the creation. God speaks of the sun and the moon ruling the day and the night (Genesis 1:16). Animals also eat plants (Genesis 1:30). So God has a concern for these other creatures. He causes rain to fall on lands where there is no man (Job 38:26).

The psalmist calls upon all creation to praise God (Psalm 148:1–10). Creation has a direct relationship with its Lord that does not have to be mediated by man. That relationship should be preserved and encouraged by man but the praise and obedience is not mediated by man. This attitude to creation influences a Christian's approach to the environment problem. It is true that man may use parts of creation. It was created for him. It is also true that it was created to serve and praise God. What does that mean in practical detail? One of the reasons such questions have not been properly explored is that the dominant scientific reductionism sees animals and plants as no more than a collection of atoms. Atoms have no rights. We can, however, make a comparison. Non-Christian political theory tends to polarize between complete freedom or complete tyranny. Either nobody has any responsibility to anybody else, nor any particular station in life; everybody is the same and there can be no authority in state, family, etc.; or absolute tyranny is allowed to anybody who by sheer force can obtain power over others. It operates this way because it will not allow the notion of men having individual covenant relationships to God, a relationship that limits their subjection to man; as well as relationships of submission to fellow men (rulers, husbands, parents). In a similar way, man's relation to other creatures has become a relationship either of total tyranny or of simply equality. Either man has absolute right over the non-human creation, or no rights. A Christian response to the question must recognize both man's position as covenant lord of creation and the animal's direct relationship to God.

THE TEXTBOOK PROBLEM

The general complaint about the textbooks produced for the

school market in science is that they are all geared to evolution. That complaint shows how domineering the problem of evolution has become. An examination will show another factor. For, despite the attempt to incorporate evolution wherever possible, and in a few places where it is not possible, evolution cannot be the uniting principle of the whole of science. The consequences of trying to make evolution your principle is that the physical sciences are left as unrelated – or poor relatives. Generally speaking, science texts which attempt to cover all of the sciences leave the impression that topics are largely unrelated to each other.

If evolution is a consequence of trying to think of the whole world as a closed system under the control of laws, why cannot the non-Christian succeed in producing a unified science text? There are several reasons. The picture of the world as a mechanical system of matter-in-motion-under-the-control-of-immutable-laws is an abstract system. It is a highly complex and mathematical system. For to begin with, the motion of the atomic particles (and to be more precise, that should involve the motion of the sub-atomic particles) has to be understood before molecules can be understood, and molecules before cells, and cells before animals, and animals before man.

You cannot teach in that way, and not merely because it is beyond the comprehension of high school students. It is beyond the comprehension of man! We have not reduced molecules to sub-atomic motions or cells to molecules, etc. The integrating principle of the non-Christian is useless in the practical teaching situation. Even evolution is not useful in this context. It involves you in so much complexity once you go below the surface. What is the relationship of coelenterates to other multi-cellular organisms? How did the mammalian jaw articulation evolve? For showing evolutionary trees and making dogmatic assertions, it is fine. But as a practical linking and integrating device, it is of little use.

Hence, science consists of a list of topics, not too much related to each other and with no clear rationale why this topic and not that should be studied.

This seems an excellent opportunity for the Christian to create an integrated course. But several problems arise. One is a very practical one, namely, there is no textbook for it. It is so much more difficult to present a course for which you cannot resort to a textbook, especially in science. It is much easier to take a secular evolutionist text and say you are counteracting its non-Christian bias. We must take a long-term view. A mile walk begins with the first step. We need to think about our own presentation and ordering of material. Certainly we cannot yet replace non-Christian textbooks with our own science texts. Nevertheless, we can avoid slavish dependence on non-Christian texts. We can make that material fit into our Christian context by selecting from a number of non-Christian texts rather than by being dependent upon the order of presentation and priorities of one non-Christian text.

There are a number of specifically Christian science texts. We should make as much use of these as possible. They do suffer from the disadvantage of being written for American conditions and of being anti-evolutionary in inspiration rather than being as positively creationist as one would like. That criticism needs some qualification and explanation. The basic concepts so far outlined from Scripture are: (1) A world created by God. (2) Within that world you have elements of similarity due to the common material used in creation and elements of dissimilarity due to the separate creative acts of God and the creation of animals after their kind. (3) That world's regularity is preserved by God as part of his patience with sinful man. God preserves the regularity by addressing commands to his creatures, for example, sun and moon. (4) God in judgment addresses different commands and will address different commands to his creatures. (5) Man as lord of this world under God may utilize this creation, but his lordship is not to become abusive and destructive tyranny. All these concerns need to inform our science, not just the fact of creation.

GEOLOGY

Let us take geology as an example of the way in which these different things can be brought together to form a Christian approach. Geology may be taught as a mere adjunct to evolution. Then the emphasis falls on the vast length of geologic time and the fossils as proof of evolution. It may be taught as basically an anti-evolutionary discipline. Then emphasis falls on the shortness of geologic time and the formation of fossils by catastrophe. Or it can be taught as a dry exercise in classification: 'Learn the names and properties of twenty rocks for next week.' It can be taught as a pragmatic discipline. That is, we are basically interested in assisting pupils to find jobs where geology is needed.

With the exception of the evolutionary approach, all of these have some defensibility. However, another way which retains the objects aimed at by these other methods, but does so within a biblical structure, is better.

Scripture testifies to the stability of the earth. Note how Psalm 119:89–91 says the earth is stable because God commands it to be stable. Note also that it is God's faithfulness that maintains that stability (see also Psalm 78:69). Part of what we are looking at in geology is this firmness that is a testimony to God's character. In consequence it must be put within that context in its treatment in a Christian school.

But God also commands earthquake and flood to destroy the earth for the sinfulness of those who live upon it. Both in biblical history and prophecy such disasters are seen as part of God's judgment, with the qualification that those so judged are not worse than those spared. (Volcanoes could also be regarded as functioning in the same way.) Thus we see in geology testimony also to God's wrath. While we should be wary of insisting dogmatically that all fossils came from the biblical flood, they do point to some sort of a catastrophe. (Why do we need this caution? The Bible clearly teaches a world-wide flood in the time of Noah during which all the land creatures and men not in the ark died. Thus the flood could have been the cause of fossils. But Scripture does not say that it was the cause of fossils. Flood geology is thus a scientific hypothesis, which might well be right; it is not a biblical fact.)

Man as lord of creation can use this world. It has been very plausibly suggested that the mention of gold and bdellium and onyx stone in Genesis 2:12 is with the assumption that man would make use of such resources. It was part of the preparation of the world for man. Certainly, we find man later using such things with God's full approval, so that our teaching of geology is with a view to man's use of such resources in his work.

However, we realize also that man is not the only creature created to praise God. Trees also sing his praise and clap their hands (Psalm 148:9; Isa. 55:12). We would not want to say that man may not cut down a tree to dig a mine. However, so to conduct your mining that you wantonly deprive trees of the opportunity to live to the praise of God's glory is another thing. Thus, concern about erosion, soil and water quality, etc. flows naturally from a realization that other creatures have a role in God's plan also.

So what are we teaching? Creationist geology, judgment geology, practical geology, environmental geology? We would not like to give it any of those labels. It is Christian geology. It is the biblical framework of thought, not merely in being anti-evolutionary, but in every aspect, that gives it its framework and meaning.

PHYSICS

Let us look at physics from this same perspective. In physics we are looking very much at the regularity of the creation that is preserved at God's command. While the Scripture speaks of God's commands to larger entities like sun and moon, we find that the regularity extends right down to the smallest entities. But that is not to say that atomism as understood by non-Christian thought is correct. In order to understand the world in terms of a set of laws comprehensible to man, one had to find an order simpler than the level of appearances. It was postulated that such a simple world of order existed at the atomic level. For many years, research seemed to be bearing out that belief. All could be understood as the mathematically expressed laws of atoms in motion. That is why the discovery of the complexity of the atom was such a blow to the hopes of science built up to that point. Part of the loss of confidence in science as the saviour of man has come from this realization of the complexity of the atom. In effect, man's hope of attaining to God's knowledge and God's power has been undermined.

While it might be pleasing and interesting for us to know the ultimate secret about the inner workings of the atom, it is not essential. We can serve God without that knowledge.

ATOMIC ENERGY

In view of the amount of attention bestowed today on atomic energy and atomic weapons, at some point we will probably encounter it. One can expect state syllabi in the future to become more concerned with making people aware of such questions. How do we put such questions in a biblical framework? Without wanting to be dogmatic, we can attempt some suggestions. These suggestions do not immediately commit us to one or other side of the debate on nuclear energy. They show what has influenced each side of the debate and hopefully provide a framework in which a Christian consensus can be reached which does justice to the legitimate concerns of both sides.

So far we have spoken about the judgment of God. We have not considered sin and God's curse upon it. How was the world changed by the curse? It is obvious that there was no death before the fall. Sin also brings with it a change in the ground. It no longer yields its strength to man. It is hard to imagine a world without death unless there are profound differences in the very nature of matter. Is the destructiveness of explosions – all of them – one symptom of a fallen world? If this line of thought is satisfactory so far, then it leads to a wariness with explosions. The hope that atomic energy will be the answer to all man's energy problems seems rather dubious. However, it does not lead to the conclusion that they should always be banned. For the internal combustion engine is a use of controlled and harnessed explosions. Explosions can, under certain circumstances, be harnessed.

The point here made with respect to atomic energy applies, although maybe with less urgency, to many other aspects of the world. The world is a dangerous place. The non-Christian is introducing piecemeal courses on those dangers – pollution, atomic energy, sex education, driver-safety education. He has no context within which to place it all. While we can place it within the context of sin and the curse, we must continue to hold fast to the faithfulness of God who has not yet destroyed this world so ripe for judgment.

DEPENDABILITY AND DANGER

We have wandered somewhat from the original point of talking about the teaching of physics in a Christian framework. We started by saying that much of our concern in physics was with the faithfulness of God who maintains a regular world. Hence, we may talk about physical laws in the popular sense as describing the regularity of creation. We may take the various engineering applications of that dependability and regularity.

Traditional science has been a secularization of the Christian view of that regularity and dependability. All was regular; all was knowable; all was controllable by man. There is in that world-view no room for a dangerous element in the world. Discoveries in regard to atoms cannot present a real problem for, if it does, man's hope of controlling everything has been frustrated. On the other side of the atomic debate are those who see the danger – but are thereby cut adrift from the traditional framework of science.

Only in a biblical framework can we talk about both the regularity and dependability of creation and the dangerous and threatening aspects of creation. For we are really talking about the mercy and the justice of God: mercy in maintaining a world in which man may live; justice in afflicting the creation with curse and judgment.

Recollecting what was said about geology earlier, you will see that much of what was said was orientated to these same considerations: the mercy of God in making a stable world and the justice of God in destroying it. We are thus pursuing the same themes in both geology and physics. Our choice of topics and our comments on them issue from our desire to allow those themes to be explored.

The bringing together of the regularity of creation, which allows practical and engineering applications, and the dangerous aspects which seem to endanger those applications, allows plenty of scope for considering the role of man as lord of creation.

BIOLOGY

We pass on now to biology. The American creationist movement has done us a service in providing texts with a Christian content. Our task is to take anti-evolutionary texts and to introduce broader considerations of the biblical picture of the animal and plant world. One such consideration has already been mentioned: the responsibility of the creation to praise God (Psalm 148:7–12). At the same time we wish to emphasize the special care that God shows to prepare the world for *all* his creatures, not man alone, and the care he exercises towards them (Psalm 104: 10–23). The non-Christian view that would reduce the animals to a mass of molecules gives them no dignity or meaning.

Too often Christians either have thought of animals in that way or have thought that animals existed merely for man's benefit. If you think that way, then you do not see the goodness of God towards the plant and animal creation. What the evolutionary mind misinterprets as the animal's or plant's adaption to its environment, we must place in its correct perspective as the benevolent action of God in creating a world fitted to his creatures. This is important because of the attempt to see ecology as a major integrating principle in modern biology. We have to put ecology in its right place.

As emphasized before, we are not merely looking at the benevolence of God in ecology. In death and extinction, we look also at life in a fallen and cursed world. From this starting point we can open up many worthwhile and practical considerations of problems in respect of ecology and pollution.

CLASSIFICATION

The theme of the mercy and justice of God is not the one integrating theme for the whole of science. There are scientific questions where other considerations will come to the fore. Take the question of biological classification. The older approach would have been to introduce the student to the broad principles of classification and to make sure the pupil knew the characteristics of the various animal groups. That tends to be replaced today by an emphasis on ecology, genetics, etc. The latter are felt to be more dynamic and less static. We have no desire to oppose the study of ecology and genetics, but a study of the variety and richness of creation is a good subject for a Christian school.

The non-Christian's real problem with classification is philosophical. The systems of people like Ray and Linnaeus were developed in the deistic atmosphere described earlier. It was held that the principles of classification were clear, rational, and obvious to man. They were implanted in creation as were the laws mentioned earlier. Hence, classification was absolute, empirical, and objective. (The conflict between this theory, sadly called a Christian theory, and reality was a major factor in the triumph of evolutionary theory.) Now things have swung to the opposite extreme. Classification is said to be absolutely subjective – 'A species is a group of animals that a competent taxonomist calls a species'.

The non-Christian thinks of total comprehensible order or total disorder. Species are a totally rational entity or they are a totally subjective human concept. We who are Christians do not have that

[136]

dilemma. There is order in creation, but not totally comprehensible order. We should point out the animals which refuse to fall into any neat classification system, for example, Peripatus and Amphioxus, in order to show that our systems cannot fit God's complexity into neat man-made groupings, but we should also point to the regularities, e.g., the similarities that bind the insect groups together.

CHRISTIAN INTEGRATING PRINCIPLES

We began by raising the problem of integrating principles in science and sketched the non-Christian dilemma. It is perhaps fitting that we end this chapter on the same note. Unlike the non-Christian we are not interested in reducing the rich variety of God's creation to a few simple principles or atoms to make it understandable and controllable. That does not mean that our science lacks unity. What unifies our science is the fact that in every area we are confronted with the same biblical truths, e.g., the mercy and justice of God; a world understandable to man in its regularity and yet a world that will not be reduced to a simple human rational system.

Thus the principles to which we should adhere in constructing a Christian science syllabus are:

1. The mercy of God displayed in creating and maintaining that particular aspect of creation: does it serve some other aspect of creation?

2. Are there any principles here that remind us of the curse that has followed sin? Will disobedience to God's law produce particular consequences here?

3. What do we see here of the wisdom of God in making a creation that works harmoniously?

4. (More specifically biological) What evidence is there here of common material with other parts of creation? What evidence of diversity?

5. How can man utilize this aspect of creation without destroying the right of other creatures to serve God?

∾ 10 ∾

Language

Usually language and literature are considered together as part of the English curriculum. That connection is natural and unobjectionable. A study of how to read progresses naturally to an evaluation of what is read. The separation into two chapters here is not reflected in a separation in the curriculum. The purpose of the separation is rather to allow for clearer discussion of the somewhat different issues raised.

By the study of 'language' we mean the study of the linguistic phenomenon of language with its phonetic, grammatical, and syntactic structure. Thus while the issues raised apply particularly to the study of English, they are also applicable to the study of foreign languages.

THE CHARACTER OF LANGUAGE

What was said in the previous chapter on order and mystery is relevant to the study of language also. As part of creation, language shows order. It has structure. Yet it is not completely logical. Languages vary in respect of the uniformity of their phonetic or grammatical structure. Yet no language can be reduced to a completely logical mathematical structure.

Thus in the study of language we are dealing with problems of order and complexity just as in many other areas.

'The Word was God' (John 1:1). We are made to think, by this, of more than the grammatical structure of language. Reason and power are also involved. Nevertheless order and mystery are both characteristic of God. There are great problems when people try to abolish the order and rationality of God, claiming that he is totally mysterious. Then God becomes unknowable.

On the other hand, attempts to abolish the mystery reduce God to the level of a man.

On a lesser scale we shall also have problems if we try to deny either the structure of language or the complexity that goes beyond our systems of classification and analysis. We have to recognize the regularities just as we also appreciate the limitations of our classification systems.

THE NON-CHRISTIAN RESPONSE TO LANGUAGE

The non-Christian response will naturally reflect the tendency either to deny a structure which is not totally rational or to impose a completely rational system. Since the balance is somewhat tipped today towards irrationalist philosophies and romanticist education, there is a strong tendency to deny the order and regularity of language. One encounters strong opposition to the teaching of the phonetic or grammatical regularities of language.

Part of the opposition stems from the fact that these regularities need to be taught to children. The child may reflect in his own speech the regularities of the language. He will not analyse it. Another has to do that for him.

Hence the romanticist, with his dislike of analysis, will argue that the child does not need to understand the structures of the language. He will further argue that the structures are changing. We tolerate forms which would have been considered ungrammatical in former times and we reject forms once considered normal. Language also varies between regions and social classes. Thus what we may consider ungrammatical may be considered normal by another group.

We see in these arguments acceptance of the rationalist idea that only perfect, complete, and unchanging order is real order. If there is any variation then there is no real order.

Yet the romanticist will appreciate the need of the child to learn to read and to develop ability to use the language. How is he to be taught these necessary things? The romanticist answer is consistent with the answer he generally gives. The child must learn not by being taught, but by being exposed. He is to absorb and learn from experience, what he needs to know about language. Hence in the teaching of reading, so-called 'language-experience' approaches are popular. In these approaches the child is exposed to a wide variety of examples of written language. These examples are not broken down into words, much less into phonemes. The idea is that the child will come to learn to read without engaging in such minute and possibly boring analysis. He will learn to read as fluent adult readers do, by pattern recognition, inference from context, etc.

While there is a recognition of a need to learn to read, there is no particular need seen to learn grammar. The child is to develop his language skills by being exposed to language. There is no need seen for any formal teaching of grammar.

A similar approach strongly influences the teaching of foreign languages. It is argued that the best way to learn a language is the way a child learns it. That is by unconscious absorption and imitation. Hence foreign languages should not be taught in the traditional way of formal grammar and memorized vocabulary and verb paradigms. They should be learned by an aural–oral method. The pupil should hear the language and practise speaking it. He does not need to have a grammatical understanding of the regularities of the language. All he needs is an intuitive feeling for the right form, the same as is possessed by native speakers.

The rationalist approach to language is characterized by complex systems of analysis and description. Behind this lies the conviction that, once things have been put in their logical form, learning will be easy. Often the result is the creation of a complex jargon to describe the order. Learning is seen as being achieved through the mastery of this jargon.

Rationalist approaches to foreign language learning tend to emphasize a formal approach. The grammatical structures are memorized, often in minute detail, ahead of exposure to the language.

Rationalist presuppositions may also be involved in the support of phonic approaches to learning to read. Often the assumption is that once the structure is understood, the rest must be easy.

A CHRISTIAN RESPONSE

The Christian finds himself unable to take sides with either position. Unlike the romanticist he does not deny order. He does not oppose direct teaching. On the other hand he does not want to teach a complex jargon to describe grammatical structures when that serves no other purpose than the learning of jargon.

Hence the Christian teacher faces a number of practical problems. How much teaching of the structure of language is really beneficial to the student? Are there other considerations which need to be brought into the discussion besides those already considered?

a) *Reading*

An example of another consideration in the teaching of reading would be that of motivation. The 'look–say' and related approaches are generally defended in terms of pupil motivation. In these methods the pupil learns to recognize a restricted vocabulary of simple words. He is then able to read simple scripts which have a carefully limited vocabulary. This, it is argued, gives him a sense of success. That sense of success will motivate him to persevere at learning to read. Similar arguments are advanced for methods where the pupil, by manipulating words in a so-called 'sentence maker', can make his own sentences. It is claimed that the sensation of being able to put his ideas into writing is a powerful stimulus.

While such stimulus is not to be denied it cannot be the decisive issue. If other methods are better, then we have other motivations besides the sense of success and achievement. For example, encouragement given by a respected teacher and the student's knowledge that he is working hard in obedience to God, are also powerful motivations.

The problem with 'look–say' and similar methods is that the abilities given the child are soon exhausted. He soon needs to read beyond the limit imposed by the memorized vocabulary. He will not always have his 'sentence maker' with him. At that point he will have to resort to other techniques. Would it not make more sense to teach him these from the beginning? An abrupt change of methods can be confusing to a child. Sometimes children work out for themselves a set of alternative strategies; some fail to do so. These latter are left confused and stranded as the class progresses to more difficult reading material. Since some are obviously reading at a more advanced level, the method itself is not seen to be at fault. Those who do not make the desired progress may not be systematically taught alternative strategies. They fall behind the rest of the class and the familiar cycle of compounding discouragement begins. Once again, the child able to develop his own alternative strategies has not been disadvantaged as much as the child who does not solve the problem for himself.

It makes sense, therefore, to strive to equip children with techniques which will take them into more advanced reading. Hence we come to a choice of a language-experience approach or a phonics approach. Alternatively we might try some eclectic mixture of many approaches. If an eclectic approach meant a thorough grounding in each approach, that might have advantages. Often it means that a mere smattering of each approach is the result. The child is left ill equipped and confused rather than confident. The common defence of the eclectic method is that different children respond to different techniques. Some learn to read in one way and some in another. There may well be truth in this, especially if the sampling of children is wide enough. For example, Australian Aboriginal children, with their high visual acuity and visual memory, are reported to respond particularly well to 'look–say' methods. The large number of words to be memorized is not usually a difficult problem for them.

Generally speaking, a consistent and thorough approach, even if that approach is derived from various sources, has advantages. What then can be said for either a consistent phonics or a consistent language-experience approach?

The general point of criticism of a phonics approach is that English spelling is not phonetically consistent. The letter 'a' stands for three different sounds in 'hat', 'hate', and 'was'. Further, there are letter combinations like 'ea' in 'beat', 'ee' in 'meet', 'ch' in 'check', and 'sh' in 'shore'. Teaching a child that 'a' means a short 'a' sound can confuse him rather than help him.

There is validity in this criticism. Some phonics methods attempt to meet the problem by introducing first the short-vowel sounds and then later the long-vowel sounds. This can create problems for children who have learned their first lesson thoroughly and had it reinforced by use. Many phonics systems teach only basic letter sounds and pay little attention to diphthongs and digraphs. This must create confusion in the pupil.

There is a way to meet these difficulties. That is a more thorough phonics system. The Spalding System is an example of such a system (see R. B. & W. T. Spalding, *The Writing Road to Reading*, 2nd ed., New York, Quill, 1969). In this system all the possible sounds of a letter or combination of letters are taught when the letter or combination is taught initially. While this means more initial memorization it avoids later confusions. The children spend more time in initial phonics drills but make very rapid progress later.

The language-experience approach, besides its philosophical appeal, is generally defended on several other grounds. One is that it is the way the child learns to talk. That is, he is immersed in a world of sound and speech. He learns to make associations and connections out of the words that he hears. He does this by context and situational clues to the meaning of the words. So the child should learn to read in the same way. Furthermore the child comes to reading with the advantage of already knowing the language. That enables him to make appropriate guesses as to what to expect in a particular context.

Those who use this defence do not seem to ask whether a child should spend as much time learning to read as in learning to talk. While reading may form a considerable part of the school day in the early years, it does not bear comparison with the time the child has spent in being exposed to speech before becoming a fluent speaker. Is there any reason why we should not shorten the process for the child by giving him the necessary phonic clues? Of course, given the child's greater age and mental capacity, learning to read may not require as long as learning to talk. Nevertheless the point remains. Why leave the child to make all the inferences for himself, and work out his own rough phonics system, when he could be taught a phonics system? Certainly, if the child has caught the main drift of a passage he can guess the next word. However, he has to read some words in order to understand the subject. Guessing from the picture on the page can lead to errors and not all books are illustrated. In practice, children tend to read the first letter of the word phonetically and then guess rather wildly.

It was pointed out earlier that romantic approaches to education are particularly hard on children who find it hard to make these sorts of intuitive guesses. Some children work out their own phonetic systems and use contextual clues well. Others need to have such things taught to them. It is the latter children who tend to fall behind and become remedial problems in a system dependent on intuition.

There is a consequence of a lack of direct attention to phonics. Children have particular problems with spelling. English spelling may have many complexities and problems. Yet it has some regularities. Understanding the rules depends upon an understanding of the phonics of the script.

Some argue that accurate spelling is not important. The children can still communicate even when they make frequent mis-spellings.

The problem with this claim is that it is a half-truth. Anybody who has read the work of a poor speller knows how often it is necessary to stop to try to work out the word. It can be read but it takes time and effort. A dedicated teacher may struggle through it but others may not be inclined to do so. If the sole purpose of education is to encourage children to express themselves, then that has been achieved even though nobody else reads his efforts. However, as Christians, we wish to teach children to communicate to others. They have a truth to convey. Anything which will make it harder for others to receive and understand that truth presents a problem. Hence spelling is important.

Another common defence of language-experience approaches is that it is the way fluent readers read. Fluent readers do not read letter by letter or word by word. They see whole phrases and predict meaning from them. Hence when reading aloud they will often substitute a synonym for the actual word. Children who read slowly, mechanically, word by word have problems especially in comprehension. They do not catch the over-all meaning. Surely, it is argued, we should not teach children by a word-by-word, letter-by-letter method.

The argument is made completely specious by a simple fact. Children taught by good phonics methods do turn into fluent readers. Many people will remember how they first learned to drive a car with a manual transmission. They tried to correlate clutch, gear lever, and accelerator. The car stalled. Only after repeated practice did they become fluent drivers who co-ordinate such movements without even thinking about it. Does that mean those learning to drive should drive like fluent drivers, doing it swiftly without consciously concentrating upon the process?

What has happened with these word-by-word readers is that the decoding process has not become automatic. It has not moved into the subconscious mind, leaving the conscious mind free to concentrate on the meaning. Obviously these pupils need to master the decoding process, which is the whole point of a phonics method.

Phonics does not necessarily produce an automatic solution to the comprehension problem. Some children do very well at comprehension. Others find it difficult. For the latter what seems to work best is a programme of material of gradually increasing difficulty and much teacher explanation and encouragement. The slower child needs slower jumps and more repetition. He does not need to be encouraged to read by guessing!

Thus a comprehensive phonics system has many advantages. But it is not the solution to all problems. Certain words do not conform to any rule. There are fewer of these than romantics claim. Nevertheless some do exist. They have to be learned. For many students the development of comprehension skills will require much hard work. Therefore it makes sense to equip them well with decoding skills to enable them to concentrate on this task.

b) *Grammar*

Much that has been said about reading can be adapted to the topic of grammar. There are those who do not want any overt teaching of grammar. They maintain that children can communicate without the niceties of formal grammar. They allege that concern with formal correctness of grammar displays a class bias. In some sections of the population 'ungrammatical' forms are accepted as normal. It is not right for teachers to impose a grammar which is acceptable to his own social class on another social class.

Once again we look at a partial truth in this claim. Not all grammatical errors made by children are cases of 'class' grammar. Some are just the results of misunderstandings, carelessness in expression, and so forth. As with poor spelling, poor grammar can interfere with ease of communication. It can lead also to the convolution and verbosity which characterizes much official speech today.

It is very hard to distinguish between differences in grammar which are purely the result of carelessness and ignorance, and differences due to effectively different dialects. For example, the language of American blacks has many of the characteristics of a separate dialect. A dialectal grammar of the language would probably show that it has its own particular set of regularities. Where that is the case schools should consider the teaching of the grammar of several dialects, not only an 'official' grammar. In other languages, it is not unusual for people to be able to speak several dialects of the one language. We should not consider this unusual in English and it may aid communication between groups in the community.

There are other instances which could not be considered part of a dialect. Australians commonly say 'meself' instead of 'myself'. It is not a systematic thing. They do not say 'youself' instead of 'yourself', though to a small extent 'me' may replace 'my' in other contexts. In this sort of situation the speaker who uses the incorrect form tends to be regarded as speaking incorrectly rather than as speaking dialect. Even people who use the incorrect forms will have this perception and will realize that it detracts from the understanding and reception of what is said. Thus this is a case in which one might explain the structure of the pronominal system as a way of teaching students to appreciate the problem in their own speech.

There are cases where we shall find it hard to distinguish between dialect and incorrect speech. Perhaps the best thing is to set these cases before pupils and warn them that their reception by certain people can be influenced by their speech. Thus they should be sensitive to the reactions of others and, if necessary, change dialect in certain situations. To do this one has to talk about grammar. Hence it does not necessarily betray class bias to talk about grammar. It may rather betray sensitivity.

If we are to discuss grammar, how do we do it? As mentioned earlier, there are very complex systems of grammatical analysis, each with its own jargon. There is no point in learning jargon for jargon's sake. But there is point in using terms which will be generally understood by the larger community, for example, 'noun', 'verb', 'subject', 'passive', etc. The use of these terms does not preclude teaching children that other forms may play roles equivalent to them. Thus students can come to understand the function of things like noun clauses etc.

c) *Foreign Languages*

One can agree that it would be ideal for pupils to have such exposure to a foreign language that they would learn the language without formal instruction. In the practical situation many of our pupils do not have that contact with native speakers. We can try to simulate that environment in the classroom but it is not easy to do it well. In this situation only ideological bias would forbid the teaching of some of the grammar of the language so as to assist the acquisition of the language. That does not mean we should adopt an extremely rationalistic approach in which all the structures of the language are taught in abstract detail before the living language is encountered. There needs to be an integration of grammatical, literary, and aural–oral approaches.

Obviously, explaining the grammar of a language is easier if the student has some knowledge of the structures of his own language. It is then easier to explain by analogy and comparison. There needs to be a co-ordination between the English curriculum and the foreign language curriculum. For example, there may not seem to be much point in teaching 'cases' in English grammar (though it may help to avoid problems with the use of pronouns). However, if pupils are later to study a language with 'case' indications for the nouns, then it makes sense to understand 'case' with a familiar language before trying to understand it in an unfamiliar one.

Obviously, the earlier one can begin the study of a foreign language the better. If possible it should be introduced in the primary school.

ᕤ II ᕤ

Literature

THE POSSIBILITY

In beginning to develop a Christian framework for literary studies, we have to try to put literary communication in a biblical perspective. For in literature one person is communicating to others; that is, the story, poem, or whatever can be understood. But it can also come to the reader as something new. It presents word pictures or a situation or a plot which the reader has not encountered before. Yet the reader can understand what is being said.

That in itself is a remarkable fact. Without having previously experienced what he reads, the reader can understand. The non-Christian takes that for granted. He has to do so, because he has no explanation for it in his framework.

We meet in this phenomenon another example of what has been previously discussed. There is order in the world. There is sufficient continuity in the world for the situation depicted in literature to connect with my previous experience. The order, however, is not the order of mere repetition. It is an order that includes newness and surprises. The reader can recognize the truth of a word picture or the believability of a story's plot while still being struck and surprised.

To understand this we must recognize the nature of our created world. It has order and yet we have not come to exhaust its possibilities. There is a great variety of potential situations which we can explore. Rationalism tends to kill literature by wanting to restrict that variety in the name of order and system. The opposite, irrationalism, also tends to strangle literature. For it leads to a form of anarchy. The words or the situations do not have sufficient connection with ordered reality to be understandable and to be plausible.

The fresh, new, yet believable simile or metaphor illustrates this point well. The comparison is believable. And it is revealing of a way of seeing things we had not previously experienced.

Language has more than meaning about it. It also has sounds and rhythms. These become proportionately more important as we move towards poetry. Also here the element of order and newness is required for a good work. Certain forms of poetry are little more than affectation. There has been such a striving to break away from traditional forms that the language used loses communication with the audience. Certainly readers desperate to be thought as sophisticated as the poet may like such poetry. Yet it requires this form of preconditioning intellectual snobbery in order to communicate. The language chosen lacks that ability.

Leaving that sort of pretence aside, we can look at the forms of literature which depend upon the sounds, rhythms and pictures of words. To some extent, how we react to such literature is culturally conditioned. For example, a cognate accusative as in 'He ran a running' sounds wrong to the English ear. Yet other languages have no such problems. Leaving factors like this aside, we still come to the fact that rhythms and sounds have to contain something of that same order and freshness. Sounds need to be put together in agreeable sequence. Rhythms must avoid both chaos and monotony.

When all these factors – sound, rhythm, and images – have been put together with regard for order and for surprise, then we have literature which is attractive in its use of words. This applies both to prose and to poetry.

If we want examples of such literature we can turn to the Scriptures, especially the Psalms and the Prophets. They display striking and original word-use in the pictures and comparisons they develop. Yet they communicate. In Hebrew they show the use of literary techniques that depend upon sounds similar to alliterations and puns. The verse is not rhyming verse but makes great use of parallelism of thoughts and ideas.

If we want arguments to defend the legitimacy of blank verse we can use the example of Scripture. Further, Scripture gives us an example of more than this. It shows that vividness of language can be an aid to communication, not a pretence which destroys meaning.

The ability to use language in this way is not restricted to Christians. Here we come back to the case of the line of Cain referred to earlier. God allows unbelievers to exploit the wonders and riches of his creation. He allows them to do things which presuppose him, even while they deny him. We have seen that the phenomenon of language can be understood only with a biblical view of creation. In his patience God allows people who do not have that view to use language. Hence in studying the use of language we shall not restrict ourselves to Christians.

PLOT AND CHARACTER

What applies to language applies also to the sequence of situations which forms a plot. We may not have experienced any of them, yet the situation is quite believable.

What we find to be believable will depend upon our understanding of man. In this respect we find a major disagreement between Christians and non-Christians. There will be disagreement on the way man acts and the reasons for which he acts. Thus what was said earlier in connection with history is very relevant to literature. For, as a creature of God, man has to make real moral choices. He will not always make the right choice. Given his sinfulness he may seldom make the right choice. That does not mean that the choice for evil is automatic. Man sins against his own nature as a creature, against what he knows from the creation around him, and against his own conscience. That introduces a tension into the life of man. The tension is increased by the misery that follows sin as well as by the mystery of God's providence in which there is no clear correlation between one's depravity in this life and one's fortunes in this life.

Truly realistic literature depicts these tensions and these choices. It uses the environmental factors not to explain man's choices but to provide the context within which the choices must be made.

Obviously the non-Christian will not see literature in this way. In the same way that he uses language without acknowledging its created nature, he may write novels that depict human character in struggle and in tension. He knows that man experiences inner conflict. He does not acknowledge that it is a struggle between disobedience and obedience to God. He will tend to see the tension as some other sort of tension. Nevertheless, to the extent that he depicts a character in tension and having to make real choices, his work becomes more believable. We can imagine somebody acting that way in those circumstances. Often, however, the non-Christian seeks ways to write about man without acknowledging the reality of the struggle. These forms of literature require special attention as there are those who would see such literature as being 'real' literature. They will apply pressure to have such works studied exclusively (or almost exclusively) in schools, whether in all schools or particularly in Christian schools.

a) *Pseudo-Realism*

What happens when we deny that man makes real moral choices? We have to see man as acting purely according to animal instincts or the conditioning influences of his circumstances. There is no struggle; no question as to how he will act. All is dreary and predictable. Plot virtually disappears. Literature becomes a chronicle of predictable depravity.

Of course, the unbeliever who wants to deny that he himself is making moral choices will claim that such literature is 'realistic'. He will strongly attack older novels which have a moral element in the story as lacking in realism or being inappropriate for today.

This then creates a debate about what should be taught in school. Is it to be literature with character, plot, and moral choice? Is it to be some modern literature with flat characters and explicit, predictable depravity?

Those who favour avoiding the depravity of the modern novel argue that children should not be exposed to this sort of corrupting influence. Those who want to use exclusively or predominantly modern novels claim that they are realistic and a mirror on life, and that children should be exposed to life as it really is.

We may grant that many modern novelists are very good at the use of language to set scenes and to describe situations. However, an ignoring of moral choice is not true realism. It does not even make for a good story as the unpredictable element provided by the uncertainty of human choice has been eliminated.

This does not mean that no modern novels should be taught. Students should have an understanding of the history of literature and that includes trends in modern literature. They should realize the connection between the denial of moral standards and the form of certain novels. Positive features in the use of language and description can be explored.

For an understanding of plot and character depiction, students have to study literature which assumes some sort of a moral choice. They need to face the question of what is 'realistic'.

b) *Sentimental and Romantic Literature*

If the denial of moral choice leads to unrealistic literature, so does the denial of depravity and evil. There is an ignoring of the struggle that every man has to conduct against his own sinful nature. Foolish and sinful actions do not have real consequences. The reality of living in a fallen world never intrudes into the fairy tale world of hero and heroine. Or if it does, it is soon and easily swept aside and the theme of 'happily ever after' is resumed.

Much poor Christian literature takes this form. It is encouraged by the superficial and lionizing biographies of Christian 'heroes' which have become popular in the church. Popular non-Christian romantic and adventure literature also has the same problems.

While such literature may seem superficially attractive to a Christian school, it has real problems. It can be dangerous in its unreality. The last thing a Christian parent would want his girl to read would be the trashy story in which a poor Christian girl meets a rich non-Christian man; contrary to biblical teaching she falls in love with him; he becomes a Christian and they live happily ever after. The reality of sinful disobedience and its consequences have been ignored. Such books tell little about life or literature.

c) *The 'Thriller'*

The denial of the moral element leaves literature bereft of character and plot. Many sub-forms of the 'thriller' try to substitute intricate and imaginative situations for plot. The characters are flat and predictable. They often have a 'good guy'/ 'bad guy' nature. Sometimes even that degenerates to the 'hero' whose only virtue is that he fights for the 'right' side. Otherwise his lack of virtue occupies a considerable section of the narrative.

Such literature is often popular. It does not require the reader to wrestle through the difficult choices with the hero. He simply goes along for the ride and enjoys vicariously the thrills, pleasures and excitement. As the subject matter of such stories tends to be about detectives, secret agents, soldiers and space pilots they have a particular attraction for boys.

Plots tend to be flat and unvarying. One could probably find repeated use of the same story line. The variety provided by real people is altogether lacking.

Some people may advocate the study of such literature just because it is popular with students. To do so would be to ignore the school's responsibility to teach and lead students. That would not rule out an attempt to bring students to see how such stories are structured and the problems which result from trying to avoid a real treatment of the human situation. As the better examples of this genre have been imaginative in the creation of situations, that skill could be profitably studied.

d) *Fantasy*

There has been a reaction against the attempt to banish all questions of good and evil from literature. A struggle of good against evil has emerged in literature set in other worlds. Tolkien's Ring Trilogy is a good example of such literature, and undeniably it has several commendable features. It depicts a real struggle and a real conflict. It shows very good use of imaginative description. The general problems of fantasy emerge to some extent in Tolkien and to a greater extent in his imitators.

In biblical perspective evil is both outside of man and in man. Demonic powers are real. Evil is also inside of man. His own nature is sinful. Evil does not reside in the structure of creation. It is quite common in paganism to make evil a part of the very structure of things.

The fantasy depiction of a conflict of good and evil can make evil a power located in the structure of the universe or in characters quite different from man. Once again, that leads to a flat characterization. Man, or whoever substitutes for man in the fantasy, may oppose the 'monsters' but he does not have to fight his own sinful propensities. Tolkien's characters are more realistic in that they have to fight their own lust for power. There are, however, pagan as well as Christian elements in Tolkien. He tends to see evil as an inevitable part of the structure of reality.

Amongst his imitators the matter is much less clear. Some are very explicitly anti-Christian. They will include Christians, or characters that are easily recognizable as Christians, amongst the forces of evil. Madeleine L'Engle and Stephen Donaldson are examples of such attitudes.

Hence fantasy literature may be good to show conflict situations and the use of imagination. Like any branch of literature it also must be approached critically.

PARTICULAR PROBLEMS

a) *Power*

One of the main themes in fantasy literature is the possession of power. The plot revolves around a competition for the means of power between the good and evil sides. Science fiction often uses the same plot, although in its case the power is advanced technological power rather than magical power.

Often the theme of power substitutes for character development and the story becomes little more than a thriller. In any case such literature raises the problem of magic. The Scripture is quite opposed to magic. Magic is power that can be in the possession of people without their needing to work for it and without obedience to God. The very idea of magic is opposed to all morality, for the person who has the secret may use the power without doing anything to justify his possession of the power. The science fiction novel in which somebody stumbles across a technological scientific secret which gives him potential control of the universe, is really no different from magic.

Magic has attraction. The thought of power is attractive to the unbeliever. That does not mean we should not study such literature in school, though to the extent that the secret of power substitutes for character it may not be worth studying. If such works are to be studied, we should make very clear the problem of magic both in life and in literature.

b) *Offensive Depictions*

Many problems are raised by literature which is offensive in the explicitness of its depiction of sinful behaviour. It may be the

recounting of profane and vulgar speech or the explicit description of sexual immorality or violence. Such literature has long
been one of the most controversial issues in education. It has set
parents against teachers. In both state schools and Christian
schools it is a most controversial issue.

The general defence of this class of literature is that it is
'realistic'. As discussed earlier, it is not really realistic. This
literature typically depicts such behaviour as natural and inevitable. To the extent that it ignores the moral choice involved in
such action, it is unreal. Thus our objection is not that it depicts
people as coarse and nasty when people should be seen as good
and noble, for the unregenerate man *is* coarse and nasty. It is that
it depicts this behaviour as natural rather than showing the
nature of evil decisions and choices, and their consequences.
Literature which focuses on the struggle can still depict people
as they really are without intruding vulgar details. For the
depravity of man emerges most clearly when seen as a sin against
what he really knows as a creature (Rom. 1, 2).

Sometimes the argument is raised that the Bible also contains
accounts of immoral acts and blasphemous speech. It is instructive to see how Scripture treats such occasions. It does not deny
that they happened. But it sets these acts in the context of their
moral character and their consequences. It does not delight in the
gross details.

In the Christian school context, controversy generally emerges
on such literature when parents object on moral grounds, but
teachers defend them on literary grounds or on the ground that
children have to be 'exposed' to real life. As argued earlier, it is
very hard to defend such works on literary grounds. The real
issue therefore becomes the question of 'exposing' children to
'life'.

It is sometimes argued that children and Christians in general
need to be confronted with depravity as part of their moral
education. Scripture knows nothing of this idea. It certainly does
teach that temptation resisted leads to growth (James 1:2–4).
However, it also teaches we are to avoid, as far as it lies in us, all
causes of temptation. We are to pray that we may not be brought
into temptation (Matthew 6:13; 26:41). Scripture also teaches
that we are not to be the cause of another person's stumbling,
especially that of a little one (Luke 17:1, 2). Hence any idea that

we are to expose children to sin in order to mature them has no biblical basis.

Further, there is no idea in Scripture that Christians must have had exposure to sin in order to communicate to unbelievers. Rather it is their godliness which is to be the attraction (Matthew 5:14–16; I Peter 2:11, 12; Ephesians 5:3–20).

What do we say to the problem of the young Christian who is naïve about unbelievers and about sin? If they are so naïve, then it is certain that we are not to place before them instances of sin which may serve as a temptation. We must direct them to Scripture which properly exposes the sinfulness of the human heart. If they do not know that man is depraved they do not know Scripture and they do not know their own hearts.

Does this mean that one case of verbal profanity or mention of sexual immorality disqualifies a work from study? Not necessarily, for the crucial question is whether the teacher can place that sin within the context of God's attitude to such sin. It depends also on the spiritual maturity of the children. There would need to be some good educational reason why one would want to teach such a work. As argued earlier, some such works may have little to recommend them as literature. Others may be more useful in teaching literature.

What we must not do is to teach certain literature merely out of fear of being thought conservative and repressive. This can be an area of pressure for many young teachers. They have been exposed to this literature in their tertiary training. They feel they have coped well with it without damage to their faith. There may even be a certain pride in their ability to cope with it. In reality it is possible that a desensitizing may have happened already. Language which might once have been perceived as vulgar and offensive comes to be seen as normal.

What has effectively happened is a change in community perception of what is offensive. An interesting example is Steinbeck, whose vulgar dialogue has often been an item in the dispute. He found some actual racist language too offensive to print. In general today, profane, vulgar, and sexually explicit language is allowed. Racist dialogue, if the character was depicted as neutrally as the blasphemous and immoral people are in many modern novels, would not be tolerated. It is not that we Christians cannot face 'reality'. Contemporary, unbelieving, literate society also excludes some 'real' language. It is that our standard of what is offensive is different. We not only find racist language offensive. We also find other kinds of language, which attack God and the men made in his image, to be painfully offensive.

Here is an area in which teachers, especially younger teachers, need to be willing to listen to parents. The parent often has a much better sense of the ability of the child of that age to discern the issues. The parent will be less concerned if a novel considered by the teacher's professor as the quintessence of the modern novel, is not studied.

This is not to defend hyper-sensitivity in parents. It is merely to argue for a community discussion and decision made rationally, with the preponderance of weight being given to scriptural arguments and the voice of maturity, rather than to whatever is popular in contemporary non-Christian literate society.

c) *Drama*

There is a particular problem raised by certain forms of serious drama. To read that play may be one thing; to act it may be another. For serious drama requires a living into the role. It means a convincing and sympathetic portrayal of the character. Can a Christian so live into an evil role?

Scripture directs us to avoid the fastening of the heart upon such things. Of course, some will argue that they can play such roles while remaining completely detached from them. That may be the case, though what is more likely to happen is that the player's conscience will be desensitized. The ruined lives, marriages, and families which have commonly been the lot of actors do not encourage one to believe it is easy to remain detached. Further, we are dealing here with children who may be far from having complete mental and emotional detachment.

Hence we need extreme caution in the roles we expect children to play. Once again there may be need for community discussion and consensus. The teacher should not assume that whatever is done in other places is suitable for a Christian school.

Comedy may have problems of a different sort. For comedy can depend upon making fun of what is good and wholesome or even holy. The institution of the family or the particular roles of parents may be subject to mockery. To point out the human foibles of people in these positions is one thing. To ridicule the position is another. Such destructive humour is not appropriate for the people of God.

CONCLUSION

Thus it is important that the Christian school should not merely copy whatever is in vogue or being taught elsewhere. It needs a positive educational reason for the works it chooses to teach. That means that some attention may be given to inferior works just to expose the reason for their inferiority. Generally speaking, however, it is concerned with good examples of word-use, character development, and plot. The work studied has to be adapted to the educational, emotional, and spiritual level of the children.

TEACHING WRITING

The romanticist would tend to argue that writing (in the sense of composition) cannot be taught. Either one has the talent for it or one does not. He pleads that to teach 'writing' is to repress the native and spontaneous talents of the child.

Where romanticism predominates there tends to be little teaching. The child writes a work which receives a mark and maybe some criticism. Then he writes another work with the same result.

What can be done? In the lower grades the whole class under the teacher's direction can prepare a story. That does tend to give stimulus and ideas to the child who is not sure how to begin. He then sees how other children handle the task and receives specific direction from the teacher.

Perhaps a pressing need is to make criticisms which are meaningful to the student. The teacher's problem is that he often lacks the time to do meaningful marking. Here is an area in which it would make sense to try to shift routine preparation and marking tasks from the teacher in order to give him time to make fuller, more detailed and more explicit comments on a pupil's work. The services of parents may be stretched thin, so this may be difficult to achieve. It is, however, a goal to be kept in view.

Obviously it helps a student if the teacher takes the time to set out how the task might have been done better. This does not necessarily take away from the student's own creativity. Often the idea is there, but he does not know how to organize the elements of the story.

Sometimes real originality has been stifled by the influence of the poor story line of the cinema and television. The boy who insists on writing yet another story about fighting and guns is an instance of this. It may take some effort to force a child out of this rut but it is in the interest of the child's true originality that he be made to develop other plots.

We could say what has been said above in another way. If literary talents are to be developed, the child cannot merely be left to learn by doing. He needs the teacher to explain what he actually does when he makes attempts at writing. He needs the teacher to analyse for him what the authors he reads are doing. He needs real encouragement, correction, and advice as he goes about the process himself.

MEDIA STUDIES

The English curriculum easily becomes the dumping ground of many things which bear little direct relationship to English. One such discipline is media studies. This study grows out of a realization that people are very much influenced by the popular media. They depend largely on newspapers and television for their view of what is happening in the world around them. Their attitude to life is much influenced by television drama and their spending habits by television advertising.

In order to protect children from these dangerous influences, many educators want a segment of school time devoted to a study of the popular media. A subsidiary argument is that, in any case, the school should be studying what the children are reading or watching, rather than trying to interest them in something outside their current fare.

The second argument we may quickly dismiss. The task of the school is to take the child into unknown territory. More serious is the argument that children must be warned to be protected from the bad influences of the media.

That children need to be warned no sensible and sensitive person should doubt. The debate is over the best way to do it. Ultimately warning will do no good unless children have a reason for rejecting what solicits them. To say that television advertising depends on appeal to greed and lust does very little good if we cannot give a reason why greed and lust are wrong.

So we come to a factor which many advocates of such courses and the similar sex-education, drug-education, driver-education courses refuse to face. These are problems that will not be solved simply by talk, as long as nothing is done to fight the attraction that the sinful nature feels for these things. One wonders if the general public are so naïve about the techniques of television advertising. The humanist when faced with obvious evidence of human weakness cannot accept the fact of sin. So he attributes the problem to ignorance, with education as the obvious remedy.

Thus the primary need is for a biblical and moral answer to the problem. If the issue is to be considered in a school context it might be much more appropriate as part of Scripture teaching than as part of English teaching.

This does not mean that we should make it a part of our Scripture instruction. There is more than enough to teach in that department already. There is a further factor also to consider. In this matter the school is unlikely to win out against the home. If parents watch television excessively, it is hard for them to restrict children's viewing. If parents are materialists, then the school will make little progress in warning against the life-style portrayed by television.

As the number of courses that humanists want the school to teach multiplies, they can easily interfere with what the school is equipped to teach. An appreciation of good plot and characterization is a very good defence against the evils of TV drama. A proper understanding of the factors involved in historical events will also do much to protect against the bias and superficiality of newspaper reporting of current events. The best remedy for these social problems is not another 'value free' discussion course. It is the school and the home each doing what it is best equipped to do.

ᣙ 12 ᣙ

Mathematics

NO NEUTRALITY

Mathematics is commonly produced as an argument against attempts at distinctive Christian curricula. For it is argued that there cannot be a distinctive Christian approach to mathematics. For believer and unbeliever alike: $1 + 1 = 2$.

When carefully examined, this argument has about as much force as the argument that both believers and unbelievers agree that trees exist or that the Battle of Waterloo happened. There are certain objects and regularities which we agree exist. Where the difference comes is in explaining why they exist. The Christian answers in terms of the regularity that exists because of creation and providence. The unbeliever denies that there is order in creation, or he tries to find an order outside of God and independent of God. It is this latter attempt which has particularly shaped the approach of people to mathematics. Rationalists have tended to have a particular fondness for mathematics.

RATIONALISM IN MATHEMATICS

One of the common forms of reductionism is to believe that the order of the universe is exclusively a mathematical order. If we had a full knowledge of that order, we would then have a complete understanding of the universe. Hence the importance of mathematics to many rationalists. In versions of this idea that have a Christian veneer, God becomes the celestial mathematician and mathematics is a way of entry into the mind of God.

It is a requirement of this sort of rationalist and reductionist thought that mathematics be a tight logical system and itself capable of being reduced to a set of basic truths. Further, there is the necessity to connect mathematics with logic. Hence the attempt late last century and earlier this century to express logic in mathematical language and to find the ideas which will unite the many branches of mathematics. The rationalist vision could not be achieved until all these were reduced to the one basic and fundamental set of truths.

Many thought that this fundamental basis lay in set theory. If set theory is the basis of all mathematics then it is logical to learn set theory first. The particular rationalist view of education demands that one learn the basic truth and then assumes that all other truths will be easily and logically derived from this. Hence rationalist mathematics teachers will think that mathematics must be made easy if set theory is taught first.

The rationalist hope of reducing all mathematics to basic axioms was nullified by developments in mathematics. It was demonstrated that mathematical systems, beyond a certain level of complexity, cannot be rigorously structured in terms of a few axioms, with every truth deriving from those axioms. Thus the history of mathematics this century has been parallel to the history of physics. The hope of physics that everything could be reduced to a few fundamental particles has received its major objection from further advanced work in atomic physics.

Many mathematical educators, however, ignoring the problems that mathematics had itself shown, have placed their confidence in set theory as the key to all mathematics and hence to the teaching of mathematics. The rationalist conviction is that if learning involves work and difficulty then the true nature of the order of things has not been discovered. Conversely, if that true order is once grasped, then there will be no need for laborious study. All will be simply and logically derivable from what is known.

The teaching of mathematics with drill and memorization of tables obviously involves work. Hence it appears to the rationalist to be the wrong approach. These beliefs meant that when set theory was introduced by the 'New Maths' as the key to mathematical education, it came with a bias against drill and memorization. There was the confidence that anything the pupil needed to know he could deduce from the known first principles. He did not need to memorize.

Against this background the problems which have arisen from the 'New Maths' can be understood. It has not proved the key to all mathematics. Rather it has tended to discourage thorough grounding in the skills of mathematics. As a rationalist system it carries with it a special jargon that has to be learned. Often all the pupil gets is a knowledge of a jargon and not a knowledge of basic mathematical technique.

In practice the discouragement of drill and memorization creates serious difficulties. Where a student has not been drilled in a new thing and learned it thoroughly, he perceives it as hard. That perception leads to discouragement and encourages guessing. Furthermore, if a child does not have the basic addition, subtraction, and multiplication combinations memorized, any mathematical problem becomes more time-consuming. It takes far longer to count out the answer on one's fingers than to recall it from the memory. Thus mathematics once again becomes more difficult.

There is here a similarity to the problem created by an aversion to phonics drill in the teaching of reading. More work early means less work later. Paradoxically the romanticist's theory is right at this point and his practice quite wrong. It is not children who believe drill is boring and soul-destroying. It is adults. They impose their aversion on the children, to the ultimate detriment of the children.

This is not to be taken as a total rejection of set theory. Physics is not wrong because people try to reduce everything to matter in motion. So set theory is a way of viewing the order and relationship of numbers with its own uses and applications. Under pressure from secondary and tertiary teachers who are aware of the problems the 'New Maths' has created for students in higher education, there is a swing away from set theory. However, given that it is a valid branch of mathematics and given that many students are still being taught it in infants' school, it is as well that Christian school students have some acquaintance with it and its terminology.

MATHEMATICS BY OSMOSIS

As mentioned earlier, mathematics has tended to be the domain of the rationalist. It is hard to point to a romanticist tradition in mathematics education. Romanticism and rationalism come together in the aversion to drill and memorization.

The concept known as the 'spiral curriculum' may derive from an environment influenced by romanticism. Or it may simply be an idea that was not carefully explored before being dropped upon poor teachers and students. In this plan the mathematics curriculum resembles an ascending spiral. Each topic – addition, subtraction, multiplication, fractions, etc. – is done at a slightly higher level in each successive year. Thus the student receives early exposure to things that prove difficult for many, for example, fractions. He receives repeated exposure. They return every year. If he does not understand the concepts one year, he may do so the next. Thus a topic is not laboured and rigorously drilled. It is absorbed by osmosis upon repeated encounters.

Such is the idea! In practice, however, there are considerable difficulties, for the student in the lower grades is introduced to several quite different operations. Before he has totally mastered addition, he is being presented with multiplication. The result is that the poorer student confuses the two operations. He may be required to operate with fractions before he has really understood the idea of division. The result is an inability to understand the appropriate operations.

A further consequence is that no one teacher is responsible for seeing that students master a certain operation; for the logic of the system is that it will come back next year again. This is in line with the tendency to replace teaching for competence and mastery by simple exposure of the children to the material to be learned. The result is that many children leave primary school with an inadequate understanding of basic operations.

What is needed is not a spiral but an ordered sequential introduction of material. The student should have a thorough grasp of one operation before he is introduced to the next.

TEACHING MATHEMATICS

A poor teacher will teach any subject poorly. Yet it is true that even some good teachers find the teaching of mathematics difficult. Many pupils certainly find mathematics more difficult than other subjects. It may be that there is a certain mathematical aptitude which some pupils have and some do not have. However, even allowing that there is such a marked difference between students, we should attempt to improve the teaching of the subject.

On closer examination the difficulties resolve into two quite separate problems. One is that on the infant and primary level mathematics is often taught by teachers whose main strength is not mathematics. Studies have shown that such teachers may give a poor presentation of mathematics and may find ways to reduce the effective time given to a subject they do not understand. In high school, mathematics is more likely to be taught by specialists. If they assume that mathematics should come as easily to all as it does to them, then the result can be just as bad. They move too quickly, give too little real explanation and illustration, and assume that everybody has their intuitive grasp of the logic of the mathematical system.

We have to recognize that many teachers are victims of their own poor schooling. At school they did not learn mathematics well. They may have grasped intuitively the order of the system but lack ways of explaining it. Alternatively, if as learners they did poorly at mathematics they may have a very hard time explaining its problems. At their teacher training institution they may have been exposed to the latest speculation on the neural processes involved in mathematical reasoning and to a wide variety of the fashionable mathematical curricula, without any concern about how one actually teaches mathematics in a concrete situation.

To compensate for a poor education the first step is to admit the fact. The next step may vary from teacher to teacher. One practical way might be for the teacher to start with very simple mathematical concepts and operations. He should imagine how he would explain them to a child very low in mathematical ability. In other words, how would he illustrate (1) the concept or operation in itself, and (2) its relationship to the rest of the mathematical system. The question of the relationship to the system is very important. There has been a commendable emphasis on the use of concrete illustrative material in teaching infant mathematics. Even so, the child has to learn to operate with an abstract and symbolic notation. Many children can understand the illustration, but remain baffled when presented with the same issue in standard mathematical notation. Thus we do not merely need to teach a 'concept' like 'addition' or a 'fraction'. We need to give specific attention to the transition to the notation. This will particularly help the child who has trouble with story problems. For he needs to be able to translate words into mathematical symbols and symbols into words.

What was said above in relation to the art of teaching in general is relevant here. The explanation should be vivid and concrete. We should use a number of different ways of illustrating the same thing, progress by very small steps, repeat as necessary, and provide ways of putting into practice what has been learned. We should be grateful for the explanations given in textbooks, but we should not use them as a substitute for our own explanations.

One suspects that this hypothetical lesson would expose several things. Some teachers will not understand the concept or operation well enough to explain it. They are going to need to ask another to explain it to them. It requires a certain amount of humility for a teacher to admit he does not know this or that. And it requires wisdom on the part of the person asked to respond tactfully and helpfully. The least helpful answer to such a request is to brush it off, on the assumption that the teacher really does know, because he is a teacher.

Experience may reveal that many teachers are in the habit of introducing a new stage by means of the abstract concepts and formal notation of a previous stage. For example, we could introduce division by saying that we use it to learn how to divide twelve apples evenly amongst three people. We would also point out that if four people each had three apples then the total number of apples would be twelve. Thus multiplication and division are the reverse of each other. Alternatively we could avoid illustration and introduce it by reminding the children that they all understand the meaning of the sign to 'multiply'. Now they are going to learn to use the sign meaning 'divide' which is the reverse of multiplication. The second way may make sense to a teacher but not necessarily to a child.

As one progresses further in mathematics it becomes harder to give concrete illustrations. Yet one can often still give analogies to parallel processes in other known branches of mathematics. Anything accomplished in that way is better than nothing.

Some students do not seem capable of grasping the concept, no matter how hard a teacher labours to 'get it across'. The rationalist would insist that there can be no progress until the idea is grasped. We do not necessarily think this way. In such cases we may have to

[166]

teach the child to carry out certain operations mechanically. That is not an ideal solution and the child will encounter particular difficulty with story problems. Nevertheless it is better to function in some situations rather than to function in none. The attempt to explain has to be continued even when a mechanical aptitude has been achieved. One does not know when the light will dawn.

ᐇ 13 ᐇ

Other Areas

If this chapter proves anything it proves that there is much left to be done. The development of Christian curricula has huge gaps. The purpose of this closing chapter is to bring together several areas which have not received the separate attention given to others. Certainly they deserve to be treated at greater length. Nevertheless the thoughts given here may provide suggestions teachers can expand.

SCRIPTURE

There is a certain amount of debate as to whether Scripture should be treated as a 'subject' in Christian schools. Some hold that it is the task of the home or the church to teach Scripture. Hence it has no place in a Christian school. Rather it should be integrated through all the subjects.

As an objection of principle this overlooks the plain fact that the school is an adjunct to the home. We may certainly argue that some things can be better done in the home. We cannot argue that it is wrong to teach something in school which is also taught in the home.

In practice there is a problem involved in the claim that Scripture is already being taught in the home or the church. It has been argued above that the school should be willing, under certain conditions, to take children from non-Christian homes. Further, one cannot always assume that Christian homes are teaching Scripture, or that the particular church some children attend has anything like an adequate teaching programme. Obviously there is a problem if the teacher in a particular subject is assuming or alluding to biblical teaching of which pupils are totally unaware.

If Scripture is to be taught in the school, in what way should the problem be tackled? Should it be treated differently from other subjects? For example, should it be a non-examinable subject? Should our concern be, not for the teaching of the doctrinal and historical content of Scripture, but for the eliciting of a subjective response from the child?

At the outset it must be recognized that content cannot be divorced from response. Under the influence of Neo-Orthodox theology which believes that Scripture is not in itself the Word of God, some church curricula, and even Christian school curricula, are moving away from content. That suits a Neo-Orthodox theology which says that Scripture only becomes the Word of God when it is effective in the life of a person. In that system it is the subjective response which is the crucial thing. There is also a general philosophical relationship between Neo-Orthodox theology and romanticism. Both agree that truth cannot exist objectively outside of the person, and that the person's acceptance of truth alone makes it true. Hence the general educational environment favours that sort of course.

We face this claim with a flat contradiction. The truth of God does not depend for its validity upon human endorsement. 'Rather, let God be found true, though every man be found a liar' (Romans 3:4). What the Scripture teaches is truth. Hence knowledge of the content of Scripture is vital. Furthermore, the Scripture contains very serious and direct warnings of the danger of knowing but failing to obey. The problem here is not that it is dangerous to know the content of Scripture. It lies in our sinfulness if we fail to obey.

Thus, as in any other subject, there is a content to be taught. Hence there is a content to be examined. We must at the same time stress the importance of obedient response to what is taught and learned. Here the example of the teacher is vitally important. That response should be demonstrated in his life.

An important adjunct to the teaching of Scripture is the memorization of Scripture. Memorization, and consequently the ability to memorize, have suffered particularly in the romanticist environment. We need to help children to acquire that ability and have them use it in storing away in mind and heart, for future use, the precious Word of God. Naturally the sections memorized should have respect to the character of Scripture. That is to say, the stress should fall upon the natural and unified blocks of material rather than upon isolated verses.

FINE ARTS

The fine arts have been a stronghold of romanticism, just as mathematics have been a stronghold of rationalism. In consequence art has been seen as the area in which the child expresses his pure subjectivity. The teaching of art has been scorned lest it destroy creativity.

The whole placing of systematic instruction in opposition to creativity is wrong. It comes from the unbeliever's attempt to be as God. God did not receive instruction before he created. Hence man, trying to take the place of God, aims at a pure creativity like God's.

In fact, when man attempts such a thing he falls into chaos and ugliness. For the moment order enters into his composition, he is imitating and reflecting the order of God's creation. Thus the teaching of order and technique is not destructive of true human 'creativity'. (Or should one say 'reflectivity'? We do not really bring new things into being. We reflect what has already been created.)

Sometimes, in opposition to the pure chaos of romantic approaches, it will be argued that Christian art should be extremely naturalistic. Even while there is nothing objectionable in naturalistic art, it is hard to argue that all other art is wrong. There is nothing objectionable in naturalistic or realistic art because there is a beauty in the things God has made. Hence to reflect and imitate that beauty is good. Yet Scripture itself contains examples of non-naturalistic portrayals, as for example in the blue, purple, and scarlet pomegranates on the hem of the robe of the high priest's garment (Exodus 39:24). Here we have a created thing, a pomegranate, placed in another setting.

There is an analogy or similarity between art and literary fiction. Neither of them can escape the order of the created world without degenerating into chaos. Yet both can place that order in settings which do not exist in the created world. Just as with fiction, the purpose should not be to glorify sin and its consequences. In a fallen world, art, even naturalistic art, can dwell on the depraved and the grotesque. We are commanded, however, not to let our minds dwell on such things. 'Whatever is true, whatever is honorable, whatever is right, whatever is pure, whatever is lovely, whatever is of good repute, if there is any excellence and if anything worthy of praise, let your mind dwell on these things' (Philippians 4:8).

One commonly encounters the superficial notion that Christian art, or the art appropriate for a Christian school, consists of painting Bible scenes. A moment's reflection will show that there can be huge problems. We are forbidden to portray God. Many biblical incidents are distorted if God is quite literally left out of the picture. One consequence of the Bible's concentration on God and the spiritual dimensions of situations is a lack of detail in its description of physical phenomena. The artist who purports to convey Bible scenes is often little dependent on biblical data.

A similar objection exists to the portrayal of Jesus. The Scripture is clear that he was God revealed in the flesh. The deity was not denied and hidden. It was revealed. John is particularly emphatic in expressing himself against any idea that the deity can be ignored (John 1:14; 1 John 1:1–3). The popular pictures of Jesus do not reflect the glory of the only begotten God. They show the long hair of a Greek hero stemming from the Renaissance attempt to fuse Christianity and paganism. And their Jesus is a sentimental and romantic figure. Unless we are allowed to portray God and are actually capable of capturing his glory on paper, we should not pretend to paint Jesus. Thus the indiscriminate depiction of Bible scenes is definitely not the way we should go in Christian school art.

While art has tended to be the domain of the romanticist, there have also been rationalistic schools of art. Cubism would be an example. It attempted to analyse figures into the geometrical shapes which were held to be the fundamental visual reality. Thus it was a form of reductionism, reducing men and animals to cubes. Our Christian reaction would be the same as to other forms of reductionism. To say that a figure has geometrical order and components is not to say that it can be reduced to those things.

Another example of a rationalist approach is the attempt to capture the essence of a historical incident in a painting. The artist may believe that the significant aspects of history can be reduced to the visible. In line with this he may attempt to depict the turning points of history as reduced to the visible. The problem is that no historical event has been truly understood without an understanding of God's purposes. And God, as we have seen, may not be portrayed.

Where romanticism reigns there is no teaching of the skills of art. The result is that the child with some aptitude does passable work. He may be forced to re-invent the wheel and make all sorts of elementary mistakes. The child with little aptitude produces works which are not what he wants to produce. He may not be able to express what he wants to draw, but he knows there is a wide gap between what he actually produces and what he wanted to do. The result is discouragement and a disinclination to express himself in art.

Especially for the sake of the latter group of children, we must teach the 'how to' of art. Here, once again, teachers may be the victims of their own education. There may be a need for teachers with the expertise to instruct other teachers.

MUSIC

Music is a reflection of our view of the world. There is an interesting parallel between our view of history and our view of music. The Christian sees history as ordered. The present develops out of the past. There is continuity. And there is also originality and newness. The present is not simply a repeat of the past. So it is also true of music. It has order and harmony. Yet it also has vivacity, freshness, and originality.

We would therefore reject the tendency of some forms of modern music to degenerate into disharmony and chaos. It is often said in defence of such music that there are still harmonies there. Certainly there will be because man the creature cannot escape the order of the creation. He may rebel against it but he cannot destroy it. In evaluating music we must ask whether the harmony is due to the rebel's failure to destroy all of God's order or due to the discovery of a harmony even if that harmony was not appreciated before.

Music does not have to be formal and classical to have the combination of order and newness. Much informal music has it. We should assess music, not by whether it is considered classical or considered popular, but by its character. In the same way that we might introduce a piece of inferior literature merely to discuss its faults, so we might do with music. The teaching of the history of music has to relate the music to the major cultural and spiritual movements of the time.

Naturally we are also concerned with lyrics. If the lyrics cannot be understood with a talented singer, that immediately says something about the composition. In rock music there is a connection between the lack of coherence in the music and the lack of intelligibility of the lyrics. Both express a view of the world as a place without order and purpose. Lyrics which emphasize the sad, the depraved, and the grotesque, contradict the teaching of Philippians 4:8 quoted above in connection with art.

We should not think that lyrics are acceptable merely because they are not obscured by a heavy rock beat. Rather we have to apply the sort of criticism we develop for considering literature. For many lyrics are silly or sickly and unrealistically sentimental.

What was said above about teaching students to produce art can be repeated with respect to music. The school lacks the time and expertise to teach everything from tuba to harpsichord. Nevertheless it should be teaching some of the skills. This can be done with voice and with simple instruments like the recorder. Our aim here is once again to help all students, not exclusively those with particular ability. In the area of vocal music we must combat the idea that singing is fitted only for young girls. Of course the example of home and church is important here also. The male teachers must set an example. Once again we may have to begin with teachers first teaching themselves. In areas like art and music there are often opportunities for parents to contribute to the school programme.

PHYSICAL EDUCATION

With a growing realization that exercise contributes to a healthy life-style, there is a tendency in the present day to place more emphasis on physical education. As Christians we could hardly object to this. We may object if too much is expected through the physical education programme. One may question the attempt to place the teaching of what are really morals in the physical education curriculum. For example, the euphemism 'health' is coming to mean 'sex' and 'drugs'. The problem of this approach is not that there is no connection between a right attitude to the body and these moral questions. The problem is that humanist educators have the connection reversed. They want to develop a particular attitude to the body so that it will develop into a moral attitude. Scripture first establishes man's relationship to God and then points out that this has consequences for the body (Deuteronomy 14:1, 2; 1 Corinthians 6:12–20). Information about the physical aspects of the use of drugs or the physiology of sexual relationships will contribute nothing substantial to creating the right attitudes to the body. If the humanist logic were correct, athletes should have a particular aversion to narcotics. Recent events have shown this not to be the case. Medical personnel should be obviously more sexually moral than the rest of the populace, especially where there are no sex education courses. There is no evidence that this is the case.

Hence we are not teaching morals under the cover of physical education. Health, as such, probably fits better into the science curriculum. We are teaching physical education with the aim of persuading children to continue a life of physical activity once they leave school.

To encourage children to do that, we have to teach the skills and techniques. Once again our particular concern should be with the child who lacks particular aptitude. He is the child who is most likely to turn into a sedentary overweight adult. He may never be a great athlete, but he can become competent at various sports and physical activities. The child with aptitude will also be helped by a course which emphasizes the skills.

∾ 14 ∾

Conclusion

Our experience of talking to people over the years about 'Christian' schools has led to some observations on the way people commonly react. There is a frequent dual reaction. On the one hand Christians are attracted by the consistency of the Christian school idea. The thought of the home and school in mutually supportive relationship is very attractive to a Christian parent. Many are also intrigued by the possibility of viewing every subject in a Christian framework.

On the other hand there may be a counter-reaction which is really the fear of that very consistency. Extremism is also consistent. So people may react to the idea of a separate and distinctive Christian educational system; or to the idea of taking the Book of Proverbs seriously on child discipline; or on another level to the seemingly radical idea that physics, art, or some other subject has been shaped by non-Christian philosophical influences. Are these suggestions no more than Christian consistency turned into extremism?

We come back to a basic issue. Are we meant to develop a consistent Christian practice? Are we meant to take seriously what Scripture says about this creation, God's relationship to it, and human life within it? We would answer that Scripture calls us to a consistent life and doctrine, not to an inconsistent blend of Christian and non-Christian belief and practice.

The legitimate fear of extremism only arises when there has been neglect of some other aspect of biblical truth.

THE CHRISTIAN PRESENCE IN THE WORLD

It is often charged against Christian schools that they are an attempt

[175]

to escape from the responsibility to be salt and light in the world. We would ask in return: when Christians in the past instituted hospitals or schools or societies where they were lacking, were they avoiding their responsibilities? On the contrary, this has been a major way in which the Christian influence has been expressed.

In more recent times the state has taken over many of these roles. Is there any reason to stand against that trend? The basic reason for opposition to the trend is that the raising of children is a responsibility God has given to parents. We may be thankful for any help the state may give, just as we are thankful for the contribution of the state to health care. Yet the state is not Christian. Its schools will not inculcate the values we Christians teach at home. More often it will attack them.

We do not avoid our responsibility to be salt and light when we take our responsibilities as parents seriously. Rather, the training of a godly future generation is one way in which we influence the society around us, especially when our schools are open to children who may come from non-Christian backgrounds.

THE QUALITY OF EDUCATION

What sort of education will best support the Christian home? Will it be education which is superficially Christian or education that is thoroughly Christian? What education is most likely to have a profound influence upon a child whose home does not support what is taught in the school? Will it be a secular education with a little Christianity added here and there or a Christian education? These questions answer themselves. If we are going to have Christian schools we should make sure they are Christian in all aspects. That means subjecting currently accepted educational practice to the test.

THE PARENT AND THE TEACHER

Of the practices which need to be put under scrutiny, the parent–teacher relationship has high priority. Certainly there are differences of perspective, expertise, and background. Scripture sees differences within the body of Christ as enriching. It also imposes the responsibility on everyone of us to use what we have for the

Conclusion

enriching of others within the body. That enriching can only occur as we are willing to listen to one another, esteem one another, and love one another.

The relationship to one another created through Christ has priority over any relationship to the world. The teacher cannot use his supposed professionalism, the parent his supposed employer relationship to the teacher, to set aside their relationship in Christ. As those who belong to Christ we must work together.

APPENDIX:
A CURRICULUM SAMPLE

Inclusion of a full curriculum would vastly expand the size of the book and might not be of a primary interest to many readers. Further, there are many curriculum areas which need much improvement.

Nevertheless, readers may be curious as to the way Christian principles translate into curriculum practice. As a sample the grades 2–6 history curriculum has been included.

Attention needs to be drawn to several aspects of this curriculum.

1. Though the specific 'History' curriculum begins at Grade Two, what is taught in earlier years is important. Earlier we teach about creation and lay a basic foundation of concepts about man and his early history. At Grade Two we judge that children are ready to understand something more specific about history.

2. The topics chosen are not sacrosanct. They are topics we judge to be appropriate to our purposes and our situation. Others, especially in other parts of the world, would choose different topics. Similarly the amount of history included in the curriculum might vary in other situations.

3. The Christian influence on this curriculum can be seen in various ways. It shows in the attempt to teach historical concepts rather than in the assumption that they will develop spontaneously. It shows in the concern for evaluating actions. The topics chosen also reflect our Christian priorities, e.g. the study of the Reformation.

4. It should be very clear that history in a Christian school is not reduced to church history. On the contrary, if we are to be a witness in the contemporary world we need to understand issues like colonization, Islam, etc. Not every important issue can be covered, but the curriculum will reflect an attempt to understand the non-Christian as well as the Christian world.

Appendix: A Curriculum Sample

Why Teach History? Christianity is the most historical of religions. The world was created in time. Man subsequently fell into sin. Through a long process often documented in the historical books of the Bible with precise dates, God prepared for the coming of the Redeemer. He was born, lived, died and rose again in history. All of history, not just that recorded in the Bible, is under God's control and fulfils his purposes.

The contention that the child cannot comprehend history, or does not need to comprehend it, is a denial of the child's ability to understand the Bible and the acts of God revealed in it.

Part of our aim in teaching history is to help the child to understand the works of God in history. However, we do not stop with that aspect of history. For history is also concerned with the acts of men who live in obedience or disobedience to God. Our aim is to help the child to understand why men act as they do and to help him to learn to assess man's acts in the light of God's Word.

THE DISTINCTIVENESS OF THE CHRISTIAN APPROACH TO HISTORY

a) The Christian approach will come through in the very emphasis we give to history.

b) There has been a tendency in some versions of social studies almost to eliminate history. Partly this is due to a belief in environmental determinism. That is the belief that man is determined in his actions by his environment. He cannot make any real choices. This view destroys human responsibility and thus must be rejected.

The world around man does provide the created context in which he acts, but it is man who has to make decisions. His decision is not determined by the circumstances. Further, environmental determinism obscures the fact that man's beliefs have a very important influence on his actions. One of the reasons we study the history of ideas is to learn about the beliefs from the past that influence men's actions at a later time.

c) We do not accept the view that a child cannot be taught about anything outside his own world and experience. This belief has also been a factor in the unpopularity of history and its

[179]

replacement by civics and contemporary affairs. If this view is correct, a child could not understand the Bible or about God.

We recognize that the child does not have a developed historical sense. We see the teaching of that sense as one of the important tasks of the history course. Hence there is an attempt to give some appreciation of the scope and sweep of world history.

d) The purpose of history is not just to point out a few great men as examples to the children. By a biblical standard many of the 'great men' are not really great. All men, except Jesus, are sinful and foolish. Our aim is to teach the pupils to recognize both the good and the bad in human action.

e) Connected with this critical approach to history, we do not treat the modern world as the correct and proper culmination of all that has gone before. We recognize the mercy and longsuffering of God in preserving the world and blessing it with many good things. We see the Christian contribution to our culture. We also recognize the contribution of human pride and rebellion to modern civilization.

f) Connected with the previous paragraph is the fact that we do not put the emphasis on human technological development as the key to history. Unlike the evolutionist's view of history, we can recognize that there have been periods of technological retrogression and there may be such periods again in the future. Technical advance may be accompanied by spiritual decay.

g) As we recognize God's mercy and longsuffering to man, so we recognize also the display of his wrath and justice. In these we see anticipations of the final judgment.

RELATION OF HISTORY TO OTHER SUBJECTS

a) As already mentioned man acts in a world created by God. This world places choices before him. Hence geography is very important for a proper study of history. Geography in turn relies very much on history. The landscape has been altered by human actions. In human geography we are confronted by different life-styles which have to be understood historically.

b) The void left in many school curricula by the disappearance of history has been filled in many cases by subjects like civics, media studies, consumer studies, etc. The aim of these studies is to teach the child to function in contemporary society. What is generally lacking in such studies is a proper consideration of the nature of man, of the origin of his lust for power and possessions, and his deceitfulness. A syllabus that does not begin with belief in a historical fall into sin cannot go to the root of these problems. They are presented as problems merely caused by technical developments: TV, neon signs, glossy labels, etc. The human source of the problem is overlooked. Our purpose is to emphasize that while the circumstances are different, these human problems have been with us for a long time. We aim to prepare students for the problems of the modern world by grappling with the problem of man.

c) Historical consciousness is very important for a correct appreciation of literature. As we study not only the material life of a period, but also the underlying beliefs of that period, we are laying the foundation for literary studies.

HISTORY CURRICULUM GRADE 2

In this grade we are laying the foundations for our future study. We are tackling directly the problems of historical consciousness. We want pupils to realize some of the ways and difficulties in finding out about things in the past. We want them also to realize that things were different and styles of life were different in the past.

In looking at maps and exploration we are teaching the geographical background to history. Thus we are showing the children how man came to discover more of the world God had made.

The Reformation shows the importance of beliefs in determining the course of history. The combination of printing and the Reformation can be used to show that the use to which a new invention will be put is dependent upon the beliefs and values of the people at the time.

Aims:

1. *The acquisition of knowledge*. A knowledge of historical facts is necessary to provide a basis for an understanding of the past. A knowledge of recent national and world history is essential to provide a background for understanding the present.

2. *The development of historical consciousness*. See preamble of curriculum to begin to understand what history is.

3. *The development of a sense of enjoyment* in the study of history and all its associated activities.

4. *The development of attitudes and values.* A study of history should develop an understanding of the ideas, aspirations, and cultural differences of people in other times and places. The student should develop a sense of history as a continuing process in which he has a place.

5. *The development of skills.* The skills to be *developed* are the acquisition, evaluation, and reproduction of information relevant to an understanding of historical issues.

Objectives:

Skills as objectives: NB. In Grade 2 we would like to see primarily the *beginning* of the acquisition of these skills which will enable the student, as he/she progresses, to develop historical awareness. Outlined below are the skills needed in a study of history. Those with an asterisk are the skills we think a second grader could *begin* to develop.

Ability to:

*1. Locate information or data – use class reference books.

*2. Recognize and recall information.

3. Summarize data.

*4. Classify, compare and contrast; including the ability to break down data or arguments into their constituent elements. (Section after semicolon debatable).

5. Use data to illustrate, or test a statement, argument, assertion, assumption, hypothesis, conclusion.

6. Test data for relevance and consistency.

*7. Understand time concepts (upper grades: to relate events to historical periods, including ability to compare contemporaneous events in different parts of the world).

*8. Distinguish fact from opinion.

9. Distinguish between supporting and conflicting evidence.

*10. Recognize motive, attitude, prejudice, bias, assumption, propaganda, fallacy, exaggeration.

11. Form an hypothesis or generalization.

*12. Think imaginatively and creatively in relation to history.

13. Formulate a logical argument.

*14. Make judgments on available evidence.

*15. Communicate ideas, arguments and conclusions orally in class discussions and reports.

16. Communicate ideas, arguments and conclusions logically, clearly and concisely in written form.

For Grade 2 we believe it is important to begin with very concrete things. We do not envisage that all that we have below has to be covered. Teachers should feel free to be selective within this curriculum to meet the needs of their particular class.

Ideas and suggestions:

Class Calendar – significant historical dates that can be celebrated throughout the year.

Suggested dates for calendar:		
	Australia Day	26th January
	Anzac Day	25th April
	U.S.A. Independence Day	4th July
	French Liberation Day	
	(Bastille Day)	14th July
	Reformation Day	31st October
	Guy Fawkes	5th November
	Armistice Day	11th November

(1 Tim. 2:1–4 – importance of praying for peace)

PART 1: How We Find Out about the Past

1. *Look at the archaeologist – how he helps the historian*
   a. Evidence in things from past – artefacts etc.
   b. Evidence in written word – clay tablets, scrolls.
   c. Evidence from pictures – paintings, sculptures.

   Materials: use pictures, make clay pot – fire in school kiln, obtain or make clay tablet imprint with Babylonian/Egyptian 'writing'.

   Looking at the evidence – what it can tell us about the past, people, way of life, ideas, etc. What it cannot tell us. The historian has a responsibility to be as accurate as possible. The further back into the past we go the more 'imagination fills in the gaps'. Stress the reliability of the Bible record as a history book.

   Activities:

   Imagine or make a time capsule: What could we put into a time capsule so that someone digging up our school in 1,000 years' time could discover what life was like in 1988. Our culture –

clothes, homes, school, transport, food, medicine, beliefs and ideals.

Discuss *perishableness* – things that will last, things that will last for a limited time and things that will perish quickly.

Concept here: The further we go back into the past the less accurate our record is. Note that one reason why we know so much about ancient civilization is that much of their record was on *stone*. How much of our written record will survive if it is on paper?

Research: This could lead into research on life of plastic, cassette tapes, materials, e.g. nylon, rayon, etc.

Problems to discuss: How do we preserve what we think, believe and feel? How do we know how people in the past felt about God, about themselves, about their environment?

2. *Look at ancient records of people's writings*, e.g. clay tablets, scrolls, ancient books, different versions of the Bible, e.g. King James compared to N.I.V. Compare modern newspapers and books.

Activities: Make a class newspaper, make a scroll. Find pictures of old manuscripts.

PART 2

1. *Maps*: Look at old maps. What did people in the past know about the world, e.g. 'world was flat'. Differences in measuring and scales. (Biblical measurements and weights – cubit, hin, shekel, minah, talent.)

   Compare old maps with modern maps – globe.

   Taken an example of one explorer, e.g. Christopher Columbus or Captain Cook. They knew about a small fraction of world surrounded by so much sea but wondered whether there was another land. Note difficulties to overcome. What discoveries did they make (e.g. Cook found cure for scurvy – importance of fruit and vegetables).

   Activities: Make a papier-mâché globe or relief map of Australia with cloth and paste of explorer's journey.

   Excursion: To Kurnell, Captain Cook's Museum or Power House Museum (museum of applied science and technology).

PART 3

1. *Reformation* (remembering Reformation Day – 31st Oct. – will be relevant here).

    a. *Before Reformation* – Scriptures were in Latin, only the priests could read the Scriptures: result was ignorance of God's Word. It was easier to lead people away from truth by false teaching. (Problem of papal infallibility. Scripture not regarded as the only or even the supreme authority.)

    b. *Martin Luther* – concerned that God's Word was not being taught faithfully.

    c. *Reformation* – began with Martin Luther's 95 sentences.
    Calvin, Knox – Reformation spreads throughout Europe.
    Bible translated into languages of people.
    Printing press – Gutenberg.
    Caxton in England.
    John Wycliffe, Tyndale – Wycliffe Bible Translators – received their name from John Wycliffe – research to find out what they do today.

    Ideas: Look at family Bibles, compare King James version with modern versions. Make a book of Bible verses for class concerning the importance of God's Word.

2. *Birth of Christ*: Historical facts – unsure of exact time of Christ's birth (some Christians have chosen 25th Dec. as a day to remember Christ's birth to offset pagan festival). Dating of calendar AD and BC – explain the meaning of these terms.

Other Suggestions

Make a class museum – collect artefacts, photos, books from parents, grandparents, etc. – from the past. Perhaps you could put a contrasting modern day equivalent alongside. The further back we go into the past the more difficult to find articles and the more valuable they probably are. Encourage parents to take children to folk museums.

Suggestions for Excursions: Museum of Applied Science and Technology. Archaeological museum at Sydney University. Libraries for old and rare books and manuscripts e.g. Mitchell, Fisher, Sydney University. Tram museum in Loftus; Railway Museum, Thirlemere (encourage parents to take children or go as

class picnic), Sutherland Shire Annual Heritage week display.
Current Events: It would also be assumed that current world
and national events would be discussed in class; that these
events be identified with the place – that the place be found on a
map, perhaps pictures shown of the place, if possible. Perhaps
important events could be placed in the class calendar to
remind the class that these historical events happened in this
year and that they were witnesses of them.

HISTORY CURRICULUM GRADE 3

Part of the way in which we teach the sense of history is by
progressively moving through history and showing the differences
in various periods. We aim to show also that the beliefs and acts of
individual men and women have been important in bringing about
those changes.

We must assess what these people did and test it by the standard
of Scripture. In choosing people with different areas of importance
we want to avoid the impression that it is merely the statesmen or
the soldiers who influence history.

A Sample Selection

Social Reform:	Nightingale
	Wilberforce
Explorers:	Columbus
	Cook
Inventors:	Watt
	Stephenson
Reformers:	Luther
Scientists:	Newton
	Da Vinci
Statesmen/Famous Men:	Richard the Lion Heart
	Constantine the Great
	Charlemagne

Further Suggestions for 3rd Class History

EXPLORERS		SCIENCE	
Marco Polo	1254–1324	Isaac Newton	1642–1727
V. da Gama	1460–1524	Stephenson	1781–1848

Appendix: A Curriculum Sample

Columbus	1451–1506	A. Graham Bell	1847–1922
Magellan	1480–1521	Ford	1863–1947
Drake	1540–1596	Wright Bros.	1867–1912, 1871–1948
Cook	1728–1779	Washington Carver	1864–1943
R. F. Scott	1868–1912	Marconi	1874–1937
Amundsen	1872–1928		
Sir E. Hillary	1919–		

MEDICINE

SOCIAL REFORM

Jenner	1749–1823	Wilberforce	1759–1833
Mendel (Genetics)	1822–1884	Fry	1780–1845
Pasteur	1822–1895	Nightingale	1820–1910
Lister	1827–1912		
M. Curie	1867–1934		
Fleming	1881–1955		
Florey	1898–1968	**ARTISTS**	
Salk	1914–	da Vinci	1452–1519
McBride	1927–	Michelangelo	1475–1564

MUSICIANS

PEOPLE FROM THE BIBLE

Handel	1685–1759	(All dates approximate)	
Bach	1685–1750	Abraham	2000 BC
Watts (Hymns)	1674–1748	David	1043–973 BC
		Jeremiah	626–587 BC
		Nehemiah	465–424 BC
		Paul	AD 35

BIBLE REFORMERS & GREAT PREACHERS

Augustine	354–430
Wycliffe	1320–1384
Luther	1483–1546
Tyndale	1494–1536
Calvin	1509–1564
Knox	1515–1572
John & Charles Wesley	1703–1791, 1707–1788
Whitefield	1714–1770
Spurgeon	1834–1892

MISSIONARIES

Carey	1761–1834
Adoniram Judson	1788–1850
Livingstone	1813–1873
Hudson Taylor	1832–1905
Studd	1862–1931
John & Betty Stam	1907–1934, 1906–1934
Jim Elliott	1927–1956

OTHER GODLY PEOPLE

John Bunyan	1628–1688
John Newton	1725–1807
Raikes (Sunday School)	1735–1811
Mary Jones	1784–1872
Wm. Booth	1829–1912
Mary Slessor	1848–1915
Gladys Aylward	1900–1970

LEADERS/SOLDIERS/STATESMEN

Alexander the Great	356–323 BC
Julius Caesar	100–44 BC
Constantine	AD c. 274–337
Charlemagne	743–814
William the Conqueror	1027–1087
Henry VIII	1491–1547
Elizabeth I	1533–1603
George Washington	1732–1799
Napoleon	1769–1821
Abraham Lincoln	1809–1865
General Robert E. Lee	1807–1870
Winston Churchill	1874–1965

MISCELLANEOUS

Shakespeare (Drama & Poetry)	1564–1616
Pilgrim Fathers	1620

EUROPEAN EXPANSION OVERSEAS

Africa: David Livingstone
      Rhodes
America: Columbus
      Pilgrim Fathers
India: Carey

New Zealand: Cook
Australia: Cook
      Arthur Phillip
Canada: Cook

HISTORY CURRICULUM GRADE 4

Empires

Power and conquest have been important factors in man's history. We tend to divide history into periods in terms of such empires, e.g. the Roman Empire. Hence for an understanding of world history it is important that the child knows the main imperial periods.

Power and its exercise is one of the main ways in which man shows his rebellion against God and his cruelty to his fellow men, made in God's image. In this year pupils can be encouraged to think about human acts. Aggression is something the child understands very well!

In the fall of the empires we see the failure of all human attempts at domination.

Not all empires are the same. They are thus a good way to introduce the child to the complexity of history. There are differences in the motives for empire, and differing beliefs lead to different justifications.

The aims of this section of the course can be related to the more general aims of the history curriculum or considered more specifically.

General Aims

1. To develop a historical perspective by teaching the child something of the changes that go on during time.
2. To introduce them to human actions that require some sort of judgment; in this case, conquest of other lands.
3. To make them aware, through contrasting ancient and modern empires, that the same questions frequently re-occur in history.

Specific Aims

1. To give some acquaintance with the Assyrian, Macedonian, Roman, and British Empires.
2. To become aware that different factors lead to the formation of empires. Thus the student will be exposed to the problem of complex causation in the concrete rather than the abstract.
3. To gain background knowledge that will be useful for under-standing:
   a) Biblical history.
   b) The Greek and Roman background of the medieval world.
   c) The problems of the modern day post-colonial period.

Structure

The Assyrian Empire is used as an example of an empire where the motive is pure aggression and territorial acquisition. That intro-duces the child to the idea of conquest. Next the Macedonian Empire introduces the fact that people may give other reasons for conquest or seek to do other things with their conquests. The Macedonian Empire introduces a case of conquest which was portrayed as a war of liberation. Hence we have with both the

Macedonian and Roman Empires the idea of a conflict of the civilized world against the 'barbarians' and of the mandate of a civilized country to rule.

Lastly, modern empires are convenient examples for talking about the role of trade and colonization in empire building. Since the course will largely be dealing with Africa, it leads into a discussion of the conflict between the colonial power and the native peoples.

PART 1: Ancient Empires

Assyrian Empire

a) The location of Assyria. The areas into which Assyria expanded: the course will concentrate upon expansion into Syria and Israel; what the Bible says about Assyria.

b) The reasons for empire. This can be introduced on a very simple level by talking about bullying and the desire of some people to dominate others. Tribute – the payments that Assyrians forced conquered peoples to pay.

c) How the Assyrians conquered. Their use of chariots and siege tactics. Deportation of populations.

d) Items that give interest and colour. Show examples of Assyrian reliefs. The class could try building a wall out of blocks and test out the various Assyrian siege techniques.

Macedonian Empire

a) A brief linking sketch to put the Neo-Babylonian and Persian Empires in between the Assyrians and Macedonians and to locate the Greeks on the map.

b) The Persian Wars. Greek attitudes to the Persians.

c) Alexander's personal crusade.

d) The attempt to spread Greek culture and language. The later results – e.g. New Testament.

e) Items for colour and interest. Description of Persian and Greek military tactics. Practise forming a phalanx.

PART 2: The Roman Empire

The Roman Empire was an extensive development over many centuries and thus shows different aspects of empire building. Our purpose is to use it to examine several aspects of empire building.

A knowledge of the Roman Empire is also important background for the study of the New Testament and the medieval period.

1. Strategic Empire. A study of the conflict between Rome and Carthage for the control of the Western Mediterranean. The basic question raised by the three Punic Wars is: does a country have a right to designate an area as its sphere of interest and to exclude others from it? (The same question arises later with the European colonial powers' partition of Africa.)

2. The City of Rome. The 'greatness' of Rome. In establishing control over Greece, Rome required the conquered peoples to respect 'The Greatness of Roman People'. Does one country have a right to claim a superiority which should be respected by others? (This is related to the claim made by European powers that their culture and moral superiority gave them the right to rule native peoples.)

3. Application in Palestine. The advantages of the Roman empire: by providing a uniform set of laws, preserving peace within the empire, developing the road system and offering to many the advantages of Roman citizenship, Rome won many over to support the Roman Empire. Empires are not all bad and may be defended by the conquered.

PART 3: *European Empires in Africa*

a) *Development of European Empires.* In order to set the context for European empire, the European expansion outside of Europe has to be sketched.

1. The explorations: the Americas and India.
2. Empires of conquest. Spanish Empire in America.
3. Empires of colonization. The beginning of British and French settlement in North America.
4. Commercial empires. The attempts of Portuguese, French, Dutch and English to monopolize the spice trade to the east. The trading companies.

b) *In Africa.* (Much of this development parallels English expansion in Australia. Wherever possible parallels and synchronisms should be pointed out.)

1. Colonial settlement at the Cape. Dutch and British.
2. The general disinterest of European powers in Africa except as a source of slaves.
3. Conflict with native peoples. The Zulu War. The whole

question of the rights of European settlement should be considered along with parallels to Australia and the Maori War.

4. The development of imperial dominions designed to secure strategic areas. The British occupied Egypt to secure the Suez route to India and attempted to control the Dutch Boers in order to secure the Cape.

5. Reactions of other powers: by way of retaliation, the French tried to control North Africa. Germans took portions of SW & E Africa. The Boer Vortrekkers attempted to break clear of British domination. British reasons for continuing involvement in Transvaal: to protect interests of British settlers and native peoples: Did they have a right to intervene? The Boer War.

If there is time, the relevance of this to the modern situation in South Africa should be discussed.

(N.B. The form of this curriculum statement may seem to imply equal attention to all topics mentioned. This is not intended. Some subjects may be treated more briefly. However, be careful not to lose connection because of topics omitted.)

HISTORY CURRICULUM GRADE 5

European colonization is a logical thing to study after a study of empires. In looking at America and Australia we are able to see the difference made by the different purposes and beliefs of those who settled.

The study of exploration links back to the Grade 2 work and shows once more the importance of the geographical background.

The early history of Australia and America raises a host of questions which require careful study from a biblical perspective: attitude to native peoples, attitude to property and wealth, rebellion, slavery, penal policy. These problems are still with us.

The child has an opportunity to see the historical context in which Australia's main political institutions developed. He can contrast this development with that in America. He can look at the influence of key figures like Washington and Parkes.

Under Grade 2 above we listed sixteen skills the acquisition of which should at least have some beginnings in that grade. These skills need to be kept in view and to be gradually acquired by pupils. Their mastery is not expected in Grade 5 but some evidence of their developing is expected.

Appendix: A Curriculum Sample

These are not to be considered as prescriptive and the depth of study will depend on the ability of class. Not all topics can be studied in depth. Here teacher's/pupil's interest will determine topics studied in depth and those studied as an overview. Not all topics studied in depth will be given equal time.

In each topic it is important at Grade 5 level to look at people in history – their influence and work.

The growth of responsible, representative government is not included. A study of local, state and federal responsibilities today, contrasted with role of Governor and British Government at the foundation of the colony is sufficient for Grade 5. There will be more detail in high school.

PART 1: America to Civil War

a) Early explorers, e.g. Magellan, *Columbus* – why European countries sought colonies in the new world.

b) Exploration – *discovery of America.*
   Rivalry between Britain, France, Spain, etc. Various countries claim territory in North America – look at French influence today in Canada.

c) *English settlers in America.*
   Take one example of 13 Eastern seaboard colonies e.g. 'Pilgrim Fathers' in Massachusetts.
   i) reasons why left England – seeking religious freedom.
   ii) why and how chose new colony.
   iii) early problems of settlement.
   iv) how they coped in new world.
   (If there is a special interest here, a contrasting colony could be looked at.)

Things to do. Research why America celebrates 'Thanksgiving' – what it symbolizes and how they celebrate. (Look at a typical Thanksgiving Dinner – remind them of food eaten in early colony.) Things discovered in America now taken for granted, e.g. tomatoes, potatoes, corn, turkey.

d) *Westward* Movement in USA – *'Frontier Days'*

Things to do. Read aloud novels by Laura Ingalls Wilder to class or study one as a class with worksheets etc., or take passages of interest as comprehension, composition starters, etc. (Correlate with English.)

Have a fancy dress-up day – come as 'Frontiers man/woman'. Have class barbecue – potato bake. Talk about:

1. Houses on frontier.
2. Way of life – farming, hunting, food and clothing, amusements. What would it be like to grow up, cross mountains in covered wagons, etc.
e) *War of Independence*. Why the American colonies revolted against Britain and how they gained independence. Look at George Washington; Paul Revere's ride.
   i) Trade rivalry.
   ii) Growing desire for economic and political independence. Inability of British Govt. to recognize growing difference in outlook – not just transferred Englishmen.
   The immediate steps to war, e.g. 'No taxation without representation.'
   Boston Tea Party
   Paul Revere's Ride
   George Washington's Army
f) *Independence* – colonies become United States of America. Brief look at constitution and freedoms it guaranteed.
g) *Slavery in America*. Reasons why slaves were brought as labourers to America. Slave trade, ships, conditions of capture and transportation, conditions in America (e.g. *Uncle Tom's Cabin* sections could be read). Look at Wilberforce in England – Abolition of Slavery in England. Civil War in America and role of Abraham Lincoln.

PART 2: Conditions in England after American War of Independence.

1. Social life of rich, poor in 18th-century England.
2. Life in English prisons, prison hulks, Elizabeth Fry.
3. Search for new place to send convicts:
Captain Cook's voyages – discovery of eastern coast of Australia. Banks recommended Botany Bay as suitable site for colony.
First Fleet: preparations
            journey out – conditions, route
            type of people on board – convicts and marines

early settlement – at Sydney Cove – problems
faced, e.g. lack of food, experience – skills.

Capt. Arthur Phillip's role in establishing settlement and
exploring environs. Contrast this with early American colony,
Part 1. Three naval governors and problems of early settlement
re food, supplies, 2nd Fleet, aborigines, suitability of colonists,
inexperience, lack of skills, etc.

Macarthur and early farming.

Rum Rebellion – role of Bligh, Macarthur and NSW Corps.

Explorers – e.g. Blaxland, Lawson, Wentworth crossing Blue
Mts.

PART 3

a) *Gov. Macquarie* – Look at Macquarie's Sydney.
   growth of colony
   convicts and emancipation
   exploration – Cox, Hume, Hovell, Flinders, Bass, Stuart,
   Burke and Wills, Leichhardt, Mitchell, For-
   rest, McDougall, etc.

b) *Squatting* – How Australia was opened up.

c) *Gold* – Look at a typical gold field – discovering of gold (when,
   where, workers).

   e.g. life on gold fields – Ballarat

   (Other colonies founded. Take one other state as example, e.g.
   South or West Australia, Tasmania and compare/contrast with
   N.S.W.)

d) *Federation*
   Important men – G. Parkes
   Australian states decide to join together as Commonwealth:
   Role of Local, State, Federal Government – visit Parliament
   House, Sydney; Sutherland Shire Council Chambers.
   Benefits of belonging to a Federation of States.

Compare and contrast with USA already studied. Note Australia
did not have *slavery* but did have 'problem' of Chinese on gold
fields.

Excursions   Visit Parramatta
   Visit 'Rocks' and Macquarie's buildings
   To Captain Cook Museum – Kurnell; Australian
   Museum – Aborigines; Museum of Applied Science
   and Technology

Folk Museums – encourage parents to take children to these, especially those in country towns.

Old Sydney Town – Gosford; Bare Island – Botany Bay; Vaucluse House; Australiana Village – Wilberforce.

Make a class museum of 'Australiana' artefacts, costumes, old photos, newspapers, books, 'Australia 100 years ago'.

Things to do Re-enact 1st landing by Cook at Kurnell (Botany Bay).

Have local gemstone club visit to demonstrate gold fossicking 'cradle' etc.

Make models of life on gold fields.

Maps in relief, papier-mâché, collage etc. of explorers.

Make up picture histories.

Have dress-up day – historical costumes. Class barbecue.

HISTORY CURRICULUM GRADE 6

As a child grows older his ability to understand the convictions that motivate actions increases. Our earlier grades have concentrated upon men and their actions, such as discovery, conquest, building, etc. In this grade we take some examples of ideas and beliefs and the actions that resulted.

The examples chosen are selected consciously. As a school based upon the biblical principles that were rediscovered at the Reformation, the history of the Reformation is important to us. However for a full picture of the history of the world we cannot concentrate all our attention upon Europe and European colonies. Hence Islam is taken as a topic to fill in something of the children's knowledge of the non-European world.

To study both the Reformation and Islam requires some consideration of the medieval world. Hence, even if indirectly, the pupil should gain some knowledge of an important part of world history.

General Aims

1. To consider beliefs and their consequences for history.

2. To provide some knowledge of religious beliefs and their political implications.
3. To give some understanding of the way the world came to be divided on religious lines.

Specific Aims

1. To inculcate knowledge of the Reformation, Counter-Reformation and Islam.
2. To help the pupil understand the transition from the Ancient to the Modern World.
3. To study, in specific cases, the connection between belief and action.

PART 1: The Medieval World and the Beginning of the Reformation

The aim of this term is not to concentrate upon the corruptions of the medieval church. Rather it is to help the pupil relate the beliefs of the medieval church to its structure and function.

1. A brief sketch of the collapse of the Roman Empire in the West. The purpose is to help the pupils realize that in times of social collapse, people looked to the church for stability and education.
2. The medieval view of merit. The merit that is gained by good works. The merit earned by partaking of the sacraments. The idea of the saints' excess of merit.
3. The relation of this to the structure of the church. The authority of the church as the repository of the sacraments and the merit of the saints. The authority of clergy, bishops and the pope.
4. The consequences: no assurance of salvation. The authority of the church over the state.
5. Luther's struggle. His life until his discovery of justification by faith. The dispute over indulgences.

PART 2: The Reformation and Counter-Reformation

1. The significance of the availability of the Scriptures. The universities and the spread of Greek and Hebrew. Erasmus. Bible translation.
2. Other Reformers and the spread of the Reformation. Zwingli

[197]

and Calvin. France, Netherlands, British Isles.
3. The Counter-Reformation. The Jesuits. The Inquisition. Edward, Mary & Elizabeth in England. Knox in Scotland. The rebellion in the Netherlands.
4. The division of Europe and the Thirty Years War.

PART 3: Islam

1. The Eastern Roman Empire. It is important that pupils realize the differences between the Eastern and Western Roman Empires; that they realize the Eastern Empire did not collapse as the Western did. The state 'Christianity' of the Eastern Empire. The inclusion of modern Syria, Palestine, Turkey and Egypt in the Empire.
2. Arabia. The continuations of paganism. The many gods. The central shrine at Mecca. Penetration of Christian influence. The Jewish tribes.
3. Life of Muhammad. His acquaintance with the Bible stories through contact with Jews. His belief in revelation from the angel Gabriel.
4. Doctrines. The unity of Allah. Salvation by works: alms, prayer, pilgrimage to Mecca.
5. The holy war. Success of Muslim armies. Attitude to Christians and to Jews.

INDEX

Absolutes: 11, 51–52, 69, 120
Academic Problems: 102
Analysis: 44–45, 64, 111, 139, 140
Atomic Energy: 133–134
Autonomy of the Individual: 10, 11, 29, 30, 47, 49, 51

Bad Homes: 11–12, 14
Behaviour: 8–10, 13, 53, 83, 102
Behaviourism: 66, 67, 70
Belgic Confession: 100
Bible: 1–4, 15, 34
Bible and Science: 132, 137
Bible as a Subject in Christian Schools: 168–169
Bible as Literature: 149
Biological Classification: 136
Biology: 135–136

Cain: 19, 20, 25, 150
Canons of Dordt: 100
Chaos: 118, 124, 170, 172
Children with Disabilities: 41
Children with Problems: 100, 101, 102, 104
Christian School Administration: 92–94
Christian School Community: 77, 81, 82, 87, 88, 90
Christian School – Extremism: 175
Christian School – Fund Raising: 87–88
Christian School – Nature: 7
Christian School – Purpose: 1
Christian School as a Shelter: 95, 96, 105
Christian School as Adjunct or Extension of Family or Home: 7, 11, 12, 14, 45, 168
Church: 3
Cinema: 159
Comedy: 157

Commendation: 66, 67
Compassion: 85
Conformity: 32
Control, Conflict over: 92–94
Conversion: 97
Corporal Punishment: 32, 70
Covenant: 23, 24, 27, 123, 128, 129
Creation: 23, 24, 46, 106, 123–129, 131, 135, 137, 150, 153
Creation Ordinances: 106, 107, 109, 110
Creationism: 135
Creativity: 30, 31, 37, 170
Curriculum: 62, 65, 67, 68, 76, 77, 83, 90, 91, 106, 138, 161, 168
  Curriculum Sample: 178–198
  Spiral Curriculum: 164

Deism: 125, 136
Dewey, John: 48–52, 53, 55, 57, 58, 59, 63, 116
Dialect: 145–146
Discipleship: 97
Discipline: 2, 32–33, 37, 53, 68–70, 74, 82, 99, 102, 103
Discovery Method of Education: 23, 51, 52, 53, 59, 60
Disobedience: 69
Donaldson, Stephen: 154
Drama: 157
Driver Education: 134, 160
Drug Education: 160

Ecological Crisis: 110
Ecology: 136
Education, Dull: 25–27
Education, Easy: 22
Education, Exciting: 25, 26
Educational Psychology: 61, 62
Election: 91
Environment: 50, 113, 114, 118

Environmental Determinism: 107, 108, 114, 117, 119
Environmental Problem: 129
Essentialism: 28
Evangelism: 56, 95–98, 99
Evolution: 48, 49, 91, 106, 107, 123, 126, 128, 130, 131, 133, 135
Expelling: 103

Facts: 18–19, 25, 26, 27, 29
Failures to Learn: 69
Family as Divine Institution: 12
Fantasy Literature: 153, 154
Fiction: 170
Fine Arts: 170–172
Flood Geology: 132
Foreign Languages: 138, 140, 146, 147
Foster Parents: 12
Freedom: 30

Genetics: 136
Geography: 119, 120
Geology: 126, 131–133, 135
Gifted Child: 39–41
God and Creation: 123, 124, 126
God as Creator: 20, 21, 27, 28, 49, 124, 127
Grammar: 140, 145–146, 147

Handicapped Child: 42
Heidelberg Catechism: 100
Historicism: 110–111, 113, 115
History: 51, 106, 107, 108, 109–122, 172
  History as Moral Example: 113–114, 120
  Patterns to History: 117, 118
  Progress in History: 109, 110, 112
  Purpose in History: 116
Holy Spirit: 36, 91
Home Schooling: 3, 5–8
Homework: 7, 80, 81
Homogenous Grouping: 40–41
Humanism: 173–174
Humanities: 17

I. Q. Tests: 37–38

Illustration: 64, 165, 166
Image of God: 62
Imagination: 153, 154
'Incompetence of Parents': 5, 14
Independence: 37
Individuality: 30, 32, 84
Innocence: 31
Irrationalism: 148

Knowledge: 18, 24, 29
Knowledge and Obedience: 35
Knowledge and Sin: 24
Kuhn, T. S.: 125

L'Engle, Madeleine: 154
Language: 138, 141, 147, 149, 150
Language-Experience Approach: 139, 142–144
Law of God: 2, 37, 112
Lazy Child: 32
Learning by Discovering, Doing, or Experience: 34, 56–60, 64, 80, 159
  see also Discovery Method of Education
Learning by Interaction: 49
Literature: 138, 148, 149, 155, 156
  Offensive Depictions in Literature: 154
  Romantic Literature: 152
  Power in Literature: 154
  Profane Language in Literature: 155, 156
  Sexual Immorality in Literature: 155–156
Logic: 161–162
Look-Say Method: 141, 142
Love: 2, 43, 54, 68, 104

Magic: 154
Marking: 66–67
Mathematics: 161–167
Maturity: 7, 35–38, 40, 41, 54, 71
Media Studies: 159
Memorization: 22, 64–65, 162, 163, 164, 169
Miracles: 125, 127
Modern Novel: 151–152
Modesty: 84, 85

Index

Moral Choice: 150, 152, 155
Morality: 49
Morals: 173, 174
Motivation: 38, 65, 104, 141
Music: 172–173
Mystery in Creation: 25, 27, 28, 118, 138

Neo-Orthodoxy: 169
Neo-Platonism: 125, 127
New Maths: 162, 163
New Morality: 49
Non-Christian Families or Homes: 98–105, 168

Obedience: 34, 43
Old London Confession: 100
Order: 25, 26, 27, 28, 30, 124, 138, 140, 149
Order and Regularity in Creation: 23, 64, 133, 134–135, 137, 148, 161, 170, 172
Order and Regularity in Language: 139
Original Sin: 31, 33, 90

Parent-Teacher Relationship: 77–78, 176–177
Parents – Their Role in Training: 2, 3
Parents as Models: 12, 15
Phonics: 142–145
Physical Disability: 42
Physical Education: 173, 174
Physics: 133, 134, 135, 162
Piaget, Jean: 49
Plot: 150, 153
Poetry: 149
Politics: 116, 121
Pollution: 134, 136
Pride: 25, 26, 32, 66, 67
Prose: 149
Providence: 112, 113, 123, 126
Pupil Dress: 83, 84–85, 87

Quality of Education: 176

Rationalism: 14, 16–27, 28–30, 35, 43, 44, 48, 51, 57, 61, 62, 63, 64, 66, 91, 118, 139, 140, 148, 161–164, 171
Reading: 141–145
Reductionism: 21, 22, 25, 129, 161–162, 171
Relativism: 11, 51, 120, 121
Repetition: 64
Rewards: 65–66
Rock Music: 173
Romanticism: 16, 17, 28, 30–33, 35, 37, 42–46, 48, 51, 54, 56, 57, 59, 62, 63, 64, 66, 90, 110–111, 115, 118, 139, 140, 143, 158, 163, 164, 169, 170, 171, 172

Sanctification: 97
Savoy Declaration: 100
Science: 17, 19, 24, 29, 49, 119, 130–131, 136–137
Science Fiction: 154
Secular Education, Educators: 12, 14, 16, 27
Secularization: 110, 134
Self-Discipline: 14, 37, 38, 42
Self-Motivation: 37, 39
Self-Teaching: 34, 38, 40
Set Theory: 162, 163
Sex Education: 134, 160, 173, 174
Sharing: 53, 54
Sin: 24–25, 27, 32, 51, 53, 68, 70, 92, 96, 97, 105, 114, 150, 152, 153, 154–156, 160, 170
Sin and the Curse: 134–136, 137
Social Role of the School: 48, 49, 50, 52, 55
Social Studies: 119
Sociology: 108, 116, 120
Spalding System: 142–143
Spelling: 144, 145

Teachers:
    Authority: 74
    Burn-Out: 89
    Determination: 74
    Esteem: 88–89
    Fitness: 71
    Organization: 72–73

Stagnation: 73–74
Training of: 61–63
Teaching: 61–76, 115
  Teaching as Explaining: 63, 64
  Teaching as Modelling: 13, 14–15, 27, 63, 67, 68
  Teaching-Style: 27
Technology: 113
Television: 159, 160
'Textbook Problem': 129–131
Textbooks: 75–76
Theory of Recapitulation: 48

Thirty-Nine Articles: 100
Thriller: 152–153, 154
Tidiness: 84, 86
Tolkein, J. R.: 153
Truth: 20, 27, 28, 35, 117, 169

Westminster Confession: 100
Whig View of History: 109, 110, 113, 121
Working in Groups: 52–54
Writing: 158–159

INDEX OF SCRIPTURES

GENESIS
I	124, 126
1:16	129
1:30	129
2:12	132
2:23–25	85
4	19, 107
4:23, 24	20
4:26	19
5:22–24	19
6:5–7	20
6:8	19
6:11	20
8:21	31
8:22	126
9:20–27	85
25:12–16	20
36:31	20

EXODUS
18:13–23	89
20:26	85
39:24	170

NUMBERS
20:8	123

DEUTERONOMY
6:4–7	2
7:17–19	122
8:2–16	122
9:4–29	122
14:1, 2	174

JOSHUA
10:12–14	123

I KINGS
11:34	117
12:1–3	114

2 KINGS
10:29–31	117
10:29	114
23:26, 27	117

JOB
38–41	24
38:12, 18, 33–35	24
38:26	129
38:31–35	127

PSALMS
33:6–9	123
38:3	31
50:3, 4	124
51:5	31
78:69	132
104:6–9	124, 127
104:10–23	135
119:89–91	132
148:1–10	129
148:5, 6, 8	123
148:7–12	135
148:9	132

PROVERBS
1:8	6
2:3ff	71
4:7	71
5:11–14	34
5:15–23	85
7:10	85
13:20	54
13:24	2, 33, 70
22:15	2, 31, 33, 70
23:13, 14	2, 33, 70
24:30–34	86

ECCLESIASTES
2:24	66
9:8	86

SONG OF SOLOMON
4:1–6   85
7:1–9   85

ISAIAH
45:12   123
48:13   123
55:12   132

JEREMIAH
31:35–37   123
33:19–22   23
33:19–26   123

JOEL
2:31   23

AMOS
5:8   123, 124, 127

MATTHEW
5:14–16   156
6:13   155
8:26–27   123
23:25–28   85
23:26   85, 86
26:41   155

MARK
7:20–23   55

LUKE
17:1, 2   155

JOHN
1:1   138
1:14   171

ACTS
6:1–6   89

ROMANS
1–2   155
1   20, 25
1:18–23   20
1:21   20
1:24–32   20
3:4   169

9–11   91
12:3   67

1 CORINTHIANS
6:12–20   174
11:22   87
12–14   57

EPHESIANS
1:4–6   91
2:1–10   91
2:3   20, 31
3:16, 19   35
4:13–16   35
4:14, 15   7
5:3–20   156
6:4   2, 6

PHILIPPIANS
4:8, 9   35
4:8   171, 173

COLOSSIANS
2:23   85

1 TIMOTHY
2:9–10   85

HEBREWS
5:11–14   35

JAMES
1:2–4   155

1 PETER
1:11–12   156
2:12   86
3:3–4   85

2 PETER
3:1–13   24

1 JOHN
1:1–3   171

REVELATION
6:12–17   23
17:18   55

DATE